The Urbana Free Library

To renew materials call
217-367-4057

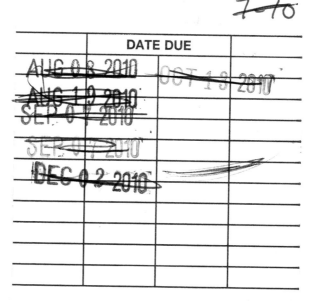

Praise for *A Kick in the Attitude*

"Good old fashioned advice on how to have a great attitude, delivered in a pithy and interesting way."

—Karen Leland,
Bestselling author of *Watercooler Wisdom:
How Smart People Prosper in the Face of Conflict,
Pressure and Change*

"Sam Glenn is known for his funny and motivational presentations and for his ability to give people a kick in the attitude. Now he has done it in print. *A Kick in the Attitude* is fun to read and filled with great ideas that anyone can use. Sam is able to mix humor, great stories, and solid common sense advice to give us a book that provides a fun way to jump-start our attitude. An entertaining read that is filled with great stories and solid ideas for giving your attitude a real jump-start."

—Stewart Clifford,
Enterprise Media

"Sam Glenn energizes our worldwide audience with his profound sense of humor and gentle wisdom, making this giant in the motivation industry powerful and approachable. He is a sincere guest that truly delights our audience. Experience his energy first hand and feel it wake you up to the life you've always dreamed of."

—Markandeya,
"Life Without Limitation," EnergyTalkRadio.com

"If there were an Attitude Hall of Fame, Sam Glenn and this book would be inducted into it! I'm no novice to books on attitude, enthusiasm and motivation, and without exception, *A Kick in the Attitude* is the best book I've ever read on how to take an enthusiastic attitude and crank up your life to a higher, more powerful and successful level! Sam's wisdom reminds the reader that attitude is a choice and that choice is a powerful emotional intelligence that transforms lives in the very moment we choose to engage in his 18 principles—and that's no mumbo jumbo! This book is smart, funny and packed with no-nonsense, real-world principles you can start implementing in your life immediately for super fast results. I'm proud to include Sam on my Life Board of Directors because he ignites passion and activates people potential like no one I've ever known. If there were an Attitude Hall of Fame, Sam would reign Attitude Rock Star!"

—**Anne Bruce,**
Professional Speaker and author of
Discover True North **and**
How to Motivate Every Employee

"Sam gets it when it comes to attitude. Read *A Kick in the Attitude* to jumpstart what everybody needs for success, a great attitude. If you do, your day will be energized."

—**Dr. Charles Stone,**
pastor/author

"No matter what your current 'drama,' the principles in *A Kick in the Attitude* will give you the motivation to turn any situation around. In addition it's easy to read, full of humor, and packed with great advice from someone who has been there and done that!"

—**Marlene Chism,**
author of *Success is a Given*

"Has the economy got you down? Is life throwing lemons at you the size of cannon balls? Then stop, buy, and read this book. Sam Glenn is 'The Attitude Guy!' He will get you thinking about you and your attitude, then guide you to the understanding that you and only you control your attitude. Last, he will teach you how you control your response to even the most sour people or difficult experiences."

—**Bob Hamm,**
Senior Account Manager, Omnipress

"Stop waiting for good news. Read this book, commit to attitude, and write your own story."

—Heather Hoffmann, M.D.,
founder of Global Initiative for Tobacco Education

"*A Kick in the Attitude* is a must have for every reader's literary library. It will lift your spirits while impressing on you how keeping a positive attitude will result in a more positive and energy filled life."

—Christie Ruffino,
President/Founder, Dynamic Professional Women's Network

"In a sea of 'attitude experts,' Sam Glenn stands alone as the authority on this all important topic. With passion and eloquence, he stands in the gap between mediocrity and excellence. Read this book! Get Re-Energized!"

—Bob Upgren,
Leadership Expert, CEO, Cross Training,
author, *The Story Teller . . . Who's Leading You?*

"Sam's book is timely. I can't tell you how many times I have spent with Sam when his inventive humor has lifted my spirits. Sam's friendship and his Kick in the Attitude personality have greatly influenced me. I highly recommend this book if you want a positive change in your life. Sooner or later, we all need a kick in the attitude!"

—Zenon Andrusyshyn,
Director and Founder Zenon Ministries, Inc.
Former 16-year pro-football player;
World record holder—pro-football punt

"Sam's energy is nothing like our organization(s) has ever experienced. I have seen Sam twice. The first time it was as our association's keynote presenter. The second time was for our MI, MPI chapter. Both times I witnessed him transform the entire audience to laughing so hard that there was not a dry eye in the crowd. He reminded us that a positive outlook on life is needed every day."

—Jada Paisley,
Michigan Golf Course Owners Association,
MI Meeting Planners International

"As the producers of the Motivation Show Conference, we are always in search of dynamic speakers and thought leaders who reinforce our message that motivated employees and customers result in higher corporate productivity and profits. That's why we were thrilled to include Sam Glenn as a speaker at our recent conference. His unique, high-energy presentation not only drew rave reviews from our attendees, but really hammered home the message that managers can get the results they want by positively adjusting the attitudes of their people. This book is a must read for anyone who wants to make positive workplace changes that will result in greater ROI."

—Donna Oldenburg,
Conference Director, The Motivation Show

"Another great 'electric shock' from Sam Glenn! Fun and fundamental—not a must read but a must DO! Sam gets right to the heart and the soul of the one aspect of life that affects everyone in every walk of life—and he does it with ATTITUDE! It's almost as fun as seeing him live!"

—Marie Hale,
Lipstic Logic Entrepreneur, Performer

"After meeting Sam and reading his book, I realize why he is known as the 'The Attitude Guy.' Sam's humor and engaging style teaches why we need a good Kick in the Attitude to unlock our potential. Success has so much to do with staying positive in the face of adversity. Let the principles in Sam's book catapult you to new heights!"

—Chuck Stebbins,
TamPogo CEO

A KICK
in the
ATTITUDE

An Energizing Approach to Recharge Your Team, Work, and Life

Sam Glenn
The Attitude Guy™

WILEY

John Wiley & Sons, Inc.

7-10
13.00

Published by John Wiley & Sons, Inc., Hoboken, New Jersey.
Published simultaneously in Canada.

For general information on our other products and services or for technical support, please contact our Customer Care Department within the United States at (800) 762-2974, outside the United States at (317) 572-3993 or fax (317) 572-4002.

Wiley also publishes its books in a variety of electronic formats. Some content that appears in print may not be available in electronic books. For more information about Wiley products, visit our web site at www.wiley.com.

ISBN: 978-0470-52805-1

Printed in the United States of America

10 9 8 7 6 5 4 3 2 1

Contents

Chapter 13

Chapter 14

Chapter 15

Chapter 16

Chapter 17

Chapter 18

Chapter 19

Chapter 20

A KICK
in the
ATTITUDE

1

Another Book on Attitude?

Yes, but One with a Slight Kick!

Long introductions bore me, so let's skip the mumbo jumbo and jump in!

Before you can grasp the real concept of this book and get value out of the following pages, let's start with a quick exercise in which you will appraise the state of your attitude. If you don't know its current state, value, or condition, then you won't have a benchmark from which to work.

Let me ask you a few simple questions. Think about them before you answer.

1. How much would you pay for your attitude?
2. How much would you sell it for?

Have you ever thought about what your attitude is really worth to you? Let's find out. We are going to place an advertisement in the paper to sell your attitude, so let's fill in the answers to some questions.

"Attitude for Sale!"

On a scale of 1 to 10 (10 being awesome), what is the condition of your attitude? _____

_____

How many minutes a day do you work on your attitude or study it by reading positive material, listening to positive audios, and associating with positive people? _____

_____

If your attitude was a horse in a race, what place would it come in?_____

Do you treat your attitude like a diamond or a pet rock? ____

_____

If your attitude was a magnet, what three things would stick to it?_____

_____

Do you let others choose your attitude or do you choose it yourself?_____

_____

Is your attitude more like an unmovable boulder or a sand castle on the beach? _____

_____

How many times a week do you complain about something?

_____

How many times a week do you laugh? _____

_____

How many times a week do you blame others? _____

_____

Is your attitude in good shape or is it lazy? _____

_____

What percentage of your success in life would you attribute to your attitude?_____

_____

What price do you want to sell your attitude for?_____
_____

Changed My Mind. Attitude Not for Sale. Too Priceless!

I think you get the general idea. It seems a little silly, but think about it. How much do you really *value* your attitude? How much do you understand your attitude and all its abilities? Are you aware that your attitude is a big part of your life or do you only think about it when someone mentions, "Hey, you better get positive!" or "Stop being so negative"?

What jumper cables are to a car battery, this book is to your attitude.

Some of the best advice I ever received is always to have a pair of jumper cables in the trunk of the car, just in case. Nobody ever really defines "just in case," but somewhere along the way, you discover what it means, and often more than once. The car battery dies and you need that jump start. Not all of us, however, take action on good insights. Meaning, we don't always act on the knowledge we have. Knowledge without action lacks power, but implementing what we know creates power. The result of not executing what we know is that we experience the "just in cases" in life and find ourselves stuck on the side of the road with no jumper cables.

I am a victim of that, too. I didn't listen to the "jumper cable advice" the first time it was given to me. I put off getting them, and it bit me when I could not get my car started in the dead of winter.

When this happens to you and you are searching for jumper cables from others, you end up "stuck," frustrated, and wondering, "What do I do?!"

Life is filled with unexpected adversities that knock the "kick" out of us. Our *kick*, as I will define it in this book, is the energy and life in our attitude. Have you ever had a time in your life when you felt like you were getting your butt kicked by adversity? I have—and on more than one occasion. The result of getting kicked around by life's challenges is that we can be drained of our passion, enthusiasm, sense of humor, desire to persevere or try again, determination, patience, courage, positive outlook, and more.

Most people who read the title of this book think, "I know someone who could use this book, or who could use a good kick in the attitude!" I have actually heard people say that out loud. I think we all know someone who could use a good jolt or kick to the attitude. In order for us to maximize more of our potential in life and work the way we were born to, we need that positive charge in life.

Now, you may argue, "Sam, I am already pretty positive."

My response is, "Great! However, I have a cell phone. It's pretty positive, too, for most of the day, but at the end of the day I still need to recharge it in order for it to work the way it was intended."

We live in a world designed to deplete us of our positive charge; Would you agree? Someone cut you off on the way to work; you forgot your wallet; another bill at the end of the month was more than you expected; someone ate your tuna salad in the refrigerator at work; your favorite sports team lost again; budget cuts; the temp stole from the supply room; your social life got boring; you fought with the spouse; someone forgot to put the dog out; the weather; government, news—the list can go on and on and it always will. Norman Vincent Peale said the only people without problems are those in a cemetery. The first time I heard that quote, I thought, "Man, I am not ready to go without problems. Bring them on!"

Bold statement, but if I have to deal with problems anyway, why not make the effort to put some martial arts into my attitude so I can come out a winner?

The fact of the matter is that it's easy to have a positive attitude when everything is good. But what about when life throws you a curve ball and you find yourself face-to-face with adversity? My definition of adversity is an unscheduled appointment to wrestle with your attitude and your situation. If your attitude isn't in good shape, adversity can whip your butt. Are you willing to settle for defeat? Or are you tired of seeing yourself and your loved ones flattened by adversity, and ready to do something about it?

Adversity will not think twice about flattening your tires and draining your battery. Adversity doesn't care about your feelings or how nice or good a person you are. Adversity is an element we all have to face. We get caught up, overloaded, uptight, and stressed out. We experience a setback at work, personal loss, or a problem with our physical or mental health. Or, life may simply become too routine and monotonous, causing us to level off and just go with the flow. As a result, we stop going for it, dreaming, creating, and becoming what we want to be. We skim by because we are tired and lack energy.

It's difficult to keep a positive and energized attitude on a single charge. No matter how positive you might be, you need a positive *recharge* from time to time. Would you agree? The unbalance of daily demands and unexpected adversities can knock the kick right out of you.

Perhaps you are sitting at the side of the road right now in a car that won't start. Your attitude battery is out of juice. You're on empty with depression, frustration, or a negative frame of mind. Maybe you've lost your job, your spouse, your favorite shoes, or even parts of your identity. Maybe life has thrown you so many unexpected challenges that you are living in fear, filled with anxiety and doubt. Your attitude has taken a sharp turn south and you feel like you are walking in a cold shower.

If your thoughts and focus are not right or not working in your favor, you need to shock your system to break the pattern or current track you are on in order to get out of the habit of thinking negatively and onto a track that benefits your life.

It's super simple. What jumper cables are to a car battery, this book is to your attitude. You don't want to be without it. Have it close by so that when your attitude battery is running low or you just need a simple adjustment or some positive mainte-nance, you are not left stranded and stuck wondering what to do, or how to get out of your predicament. It will ensure that you get and keep a positively charged life. In order to thrive despite whatever comes our way, we need to keep that positive charge strong. This is what it means to get a kick in the attitude.

It seems everyone is on the lookout for the "New Thing," be it a concept, a secret, or a foolproof formula for happiness and success. Let me point out up front, what you are about to read is not anything new. I don't have any secrets for you or special formulas. I will instead simply give you my perspective, a fresh presentation of material that has been around for thousands of years. So why read something old?

My stuff is old school. But it works, and was designed specifically for you.

I am guessing a lot of people will struggle with the simplicity of my message because we live in a time when we tend to overcomplicate things. But why would you look for that concept to change "everything" in your life when you have diamonds of information all around you that simply need to be unearthed?

I'm going to take you back to the basics that work, creating achievement, success, and happiness. The process will be entertaining and interactive. I didn't spend years writing, studying, researching, and investing my life to bore you, but rather to inspire you.

This book just happens to be my perspective and it may or may not be one with which you connect. If you don't, it's not my fault or yours. It is what it is.

If we know a positive attitude can make life better, then why doesn't everyone have one?

Hmmmmm. . . .

Let's face it, "attitude" isn't rocket science, yet if we know a positive attitude can make life better, then why doesn't everyone have one? It's simple. Either:

• People don't care.
• People don't get it.

- People see insufficient intrinsic value in their attitudes to
  work on them daily, instead ignoring their assets as it
  collects dust and wastes away.

A concept I learned from Dr. William Glasser is that all life
will ever give you is information and how you interpret that
information determines your outcome, feelings, and experiences. In his book *Choice Theory*, he teaches people how to take
responsibility for their own lives, rather than trying to control
the lives of others. A better attitude will create a better inter-
pretation of life's information, which will completely change
your life. You don't need a secret concept. You simply need to be
aware of the power of your attitude, and realize how to charge it
and keep it charged. You need to relearn the basics so that you
can thrive.

In the book, I may seem like I am saying the same thing
over and over again, but the purpose is to condition your mind
so you get it, got it, and then live it.

When I played basketball, my coach never shared a newly
released concept to improve the way we played, but he did stick
with what works—core fundamentals. And it wasn't enough to
know them; we had to do what we knew. That's why so many
people struggle today. They know what they need to do to
change their lives for the better, but they don't do what they
know. The reason again is that they don't care enough, are too
lazy, or just don't get it. This book is about putting what you
know into positive action.

The core fundamentals of success haven't changed with
time and no matter what your circumstance is, they can still
work for you to get the results you want. Why do you think
"fundamentals" were the key to success for former UCLA
basketball coach John Wooden, who won 19 NCAA conference

championships? He won with clearly defined fundamentals put into action. He didn't reinvent the wheel each new season when he got new players with unique personalities, backgrounds, and challenges. He applied what works and moves people toward success—the fundamentals. Are your core fundamentals for achieving your desired goals clearly defined? Do you need to review them, update them, and examine where you apply them? Remember, the seasons will change, but the fundamentals work the same way in all seasons.

I am not saying that my way is the only way. I am offering some ideas that I have found that work. If you can get one good idea out of this book that will set your attitude in a positive direction, ignite your passion, get you the result you want, would that be worth it for you?

The initial manuscript of this book was written for one person—*me*! It was actually my journal. I found that I was often referring to the notes and realizing something new every time I read the same material. I forget things easily, so I created something to remind me of the attitude fundamentals. That way, if I ever got off track, I would have a guide to bring me back—bread crumbs, so to speak. What turned my personal journal into a book? you might ask. I met other people who needed that positive charge for their attitudes, and so I shared my notebook of attitude fundamentals. They shared it with others, and so on, until it became like a positive virus that was healing negative attitudes everywhere.

I should also quickly mention up front, I have an intense case of ADD (attention deficit disorder). I don't take medication. I just live with the entertainment of what I have. An ADDer pays attention to the most sparkly thing in the room. And books these days are not always ADD friendly. They might have a cool looking cover and title, but then you open them up and you're like, "Oh, man . . . work!" You think, "I will get to it another time," and yet you never do.

I remember appearing at an event years ago during which the introduction for a motivational speaker preceding me included the statement that he had read 700 books. (I think it was to build credibility. Who knows?) I thought, "Wow. I have tried to read 700 books, but they didn't have sticking power."

Just for fun, I changed up my introduction and told the audience, "I am sorry; I haven't read 700 books, but I did listen to the first speaker read his 700 books out loud." It got a good laugh.

Isn't it frustrating when you buy a book, and after reading a few pages, you begin to think about what you need to get at the store, or who you forgot to call back, or why the earth is round? We all have that distractibility to a degree, but multiply it, and you have ADD. I like to cater to my fellow ADDers, and I think you will get a kick out of it as well, even if you don't have ADD. I don't want to waste time, and I want this information to stick, so there are surprises along the way to keep you engaged. My book is what I call "ADD friendly."

Along those lines, I had an e-mail from a 12-year-old girl recently, and here is what she said: "Dear Sam, I am twelve years old and the reason I am writing is about your book. I got into some trouble at school and was grounded to my room. No TV. No Internet. No nothing. My mom handed me your book to read while I was grounded, and I just threw it across the room. I sat there for hours, and then for some reason, I picked it up to flip through it. At first, I thought, 'Another book to read . . . Ahhh!' Then I started to read your stories about falling off the airplane and having toilet paper stuck to your pants and I started laughing so hard and loud, my mom thought I was watching TV and came in my room to scold me. But I showed her I was reading your book, and I finished it. Not only that, I have reread it and keep it on my nightstand. I told all my friends about you and that they need to get your book. This book has changed my life. I don't get in trouble anymore, and I have a better focus of what I want in life. Also, I think you are funny."

How do you respond when you get a book on the subject of attitude put before you? Even if we don't physically throw it across the room, we often do so mentally. To counteract that desire, I've tried to make this book as fun and easy to swallow as possible.

Maybe you live with someone who is highly negative and you are very positive and you battle thoughts on, "What can I do?" Or you may be a manager, or someone who would like to influence others . . .

A lot of times, we want to change people, but we can't, no matter how hard we try. It's frustrating . . . I know. It's like the old saying goes, "You can lead a horse to the water, but you can't force the horse to drink." One of my goals in this book is to give you some hope about how to teach people to drink something good. If that doesn't work, then maybe you could gift them this book, or a Happy Meal (more on that later).

A couple more practical details. You don't have to read this book all at once. You don't eat a whole buffet of good food at one sitting, do you? No. You keep coming back for more to nurture your body when you are hungry and need a boost.

Mark Up This Book

Underline what you like. Write notes in the margins. Think about what you read and let it soak in, then make it yours. I left room in the back of the book for you to scribble, doodle, and write your reflections. You can also answer the Attitude in Action questions here, which are posted at the end of each chapter (but I also have questions throughout some of the chapters, so keep your eye out for opportunities to write).

If you are taking yourself seriously, get yourself a spiral-bound journal. It's the easiest kind to lay on the table.

Now . . . take in a nice, deep breath, and allow yourself to embrace the experience that these pages are ready to create for you. Stop every now and then to reflect on your life, because this is all about you. Think about where you are, where you want to go, and what you need to get there. Jot down your own ideas. When you put this book down and go back to your daily activities, I want you to feel energized and empowered. I want you to find your kick, use it, and keep it.

Attitude in Action

How much is your attitude truly worth? Do the attitude-for-sale exercise earlier in this chapter, and write your answers at the end of the book or in your journal.

Participate in the "Attitude Works" Movement. Go to EverythingAttitude.com and join thousands who have declared that Attitude Works. If you have a story of how attitude has worked in your life, e-mail it to us.

2

How a Kick in the Attitude Transformed a Negative, Uptight, Complaining, Blaming, Depressed Man into "The Attitude Guy™"

It is said a journey is not about what you get, but rather who you become along the way. I have had the privilege of speaking to organizations on the value of attitude for close to 14 years, so from time to time, I get recognized. No one ever remembers my birth name, "Sam." Instead, a few years back I began to notice a trend. I was walking through Chicago O'Hare airport and someone yelled out pretty loudly, "Hey, it's The Attitude Guy!"

Being the naive person I am, I started looking around like a kid in a candy shop. "Hey. I want to see The Attitude Guy! Where is he?!"

I was glancing all over and then noticed everyone was looking at me. Was I The Attitude Guy? Or was my zipper down again and I didn't know it?

The person who had yelled ran up to me with a group of people and enthusiastically said, "Hey, I know you! You're The Attitude Guy! You spoke at our company conference. We laughed so hard, my supervisor peed her pants."

All I could say was, "That's awesome! I am glad I could create that impact for you guys and make someone wet herself."

It's hard to believe looking back that I was once a negative, uptight, complaining, blaming, and depressed man. Now, I have the good fortune to help people on a subject that I am so passionate about—Attitude. And as a special bonus, I found this amazing sense of humor within myself that I love to share with my audiences, family, and friends. To say my audiences laugh politely would be a huge understatement. I am not exaggerating, but I have had people laugh so hard they have passed out, wet themselves, cried, fallen out of their chairs, run to the bathroom, and had stomachaches and sore cheeks for days. And folks, I am by no means a comedian. I am just real, relatable, and people find my stories humorous.

To be a source for helping people switch the light on within themselves is truly an honor, considering I never set out to be a professional speaker. I am shy and highly introverted. But, when you discover your purpose, it has a way of calling you until you do it, and once you go for it, life can never be the same.

My journey led me to become known as The Attitude Guy. I didn't create that title. It's just what people call me when they introduce me, or see me in airports or in passing. It's important for you to understand that I didn't just slap a name on myself for the purpose of creative marketing. However, it does work and fits well with my passion. I value and respect the power of attitude. It's a gift we are born with that, when utilized properly in all its awesome power, will bring the harvest of rewards that life has to offer. For this reason, I have become what I live and talk about.

My title, however, didn't come easily. Sometimes we have to learn our lessons the hard way, and not always by choice. I did.

In 1997, I encountered some pretty hefty challenges that put my attitude to the test. I had been operating a small but successful business that my grandfather had run for more than 30 years before entrusting it to our family, which I more or less just took over. We distributed wild bird products. You may have seen some of these items, like birdhouses and birdseed. You may find it interesting that birding is the number-two hobby in the world (second only to gardening). For real! I was honored to take this mantle from my grandfather and carry it. I was charged with feelings of importance, like I was on my way. (I just didn't realize I was on my way to something other than what I'd chosen.)

Running the business was hard work. I invested years as well as a lot of sacrifice and money into it. Just when I thought things would finally be kicking into high gear, I got an un-scheduled appointment with adversity. It came in the form of a phone call informing me that the warehouse which assembled, stored, and shipped our products had gone up in flames.

At first I thought it was a joke. Nope, it was reality.

You might think, "Well, you had insurance, right?" Wrong. Every kind offered, except this one. The business utilized subcontracted work, so it didn't require me to have fire insurance. As a result, my name was on everything and in a moment I had lost it all. I had lost my grandfather's 30-year-old company, which he had used to fund family Christmas gifts, travel, and life fulfillment with his wife, my grandma.

I think if my grandfather were alive, however, he would have said, "I left behind a final gift just for you, Sam."

You might be thinking, "A gift? Are you kidding?"

Attitude Kicker

It may not seem like a gift or opportunity when life changes in such a way, but the difference between setback and opportunities resides in one word, "attitude." Life offers us gifts, we just open them at different times. They may come in the form of a life-changing experience.

When all this happened, I was devastated. I felt like I had let down my entire family, and like my own life and success had come to a permanent stop.

For several years after this incident, I became like a drifter. I had no direction. My attitude battery was on empty. I was hitchhiking my way through life. When the company went under, I went with it. I wallowed in self-pity, and found myself engaging in bad habits like sleeping all day, overeating, and trying to play the lottery to get back into the game of life. Looking back, however, this hardship was the best thing that could have happened to me.

Thankfully, my mom was generous enough to let me stay with her for a brief while. My parents had divorced a short time before and she could only afford to live in a one bedroom apartment. I basically camped out on the living room floor in a sleeping bag, except it wasn't much like camping—there were no marshmallows or camp songs. It was incredibly humbling, to say the least. I felt like the biggest loser.

I needed to make some money to get by. Since I didn't know where to start or what to do, I applied for a few night jobs—the graveyard shift. Working the graveyard shift is not easy. I tip my hat to anyone who does. I delivered newspapers at 2:00 A.M., and eventually got some work as a nighttime cleanup guy. I mainly scrubbed floors and did janitorial work.

During that time, I struggled with my self-esteem, having gone from successful business owner to nighttime janitor and newspaper delivery guy. Now mind you, there is nothing wrong with those vocations, but Earl Nightingale, who was a motivational speaker, radio host and author as well as one of the 12 surviving Marines on board the USS Arizona during the attack on Pearl Harbor, defines success as the realization of a worthy ideal. If you are doing what you want to do and doing it with purpose, then it's success. Folks, I didn't like getting up in the middle of the night to deliver the news or clean someone's bathroom. I struggled to see the "worthy ideal" in my job.

Still, I did it. I put my ego aside and worked. Let me also admit that the gravitational pull to become negative was intense. My circumstances provided me with every reason or excuse to justify a foul and defeatist outlook.

The Cup of Coffee That Changed My Attitude for Life!

I was struggling to make a dollar and pay people back. One day my good friend, Andy Warcaba, invited me down the street to a small coffee shop to talk. I was all for it. I enjoy a good cup of coffee in the company of friends. What Andy shared with me, however, wasn't exactly what I wanted to hear. But it was what I needed to hear. The difference between hearing and listening is that if you just hear it, it can go in one ear and out the other. When you listen, you absorb and can apply the information to your attitude and actions. I listened.

In simple terms, he told me, "Sam, you don't have a hard-knock life problem. What you have is an attitude problem."

Those are shocking words that often require a spoonful of sugar so they go down easy. I got what best-selling author Larry Winget calls "the ugly truth."

It was true. I was living with a broken-down attitude; and that was my fault. My life was a miserable reflection of my attitude. And it wasn't pretty. Broken attitudes don't paint rainbows. They just attract more brokenness.

You have probably heard the saying, "The truth will set you free." I believe the truth will set you free, but only if you buy into the truth as real, acknowledge the value of it, and do something about it. Take action!

My ego was bruised a bit by the ugly truth, but since I couldn't afford to pay for the coffee, I was humbled enough to listen as my good friend encouraged me and, like a car battery that has just gotten a jump-start, my attitude kicked into gear. I began to see the value in what he was saying. We spent the next hour writing lists of all the things for which I was thankful in my life. Initially, that activity may have seemed like a waste of time, but it put me on the fast track to some real perspective. My perspective on life, at the time, was that I was the victim and everyone was to blame. Bottom line, I wasn't accepting responsibility for my life, even though I was its sole owner.

If things are not working out your way, you can't move forward by blaming others. Sometimes, it won't be your fault.

But the moment you blame, you give away all your power to do anything about it.

At first, when Andy asked what I had to be grateful for, I was like, "I need to think about that for a while." You should never have to think about what you have to be thankful for. It should always be at the front of your mind.

Andy assisted me in the exercise, and we started small. Some of the things we came up with made me laugh, like toothbrushes and underwear. I was slowly taking responsibility for my life and putting my attitude into action. By the time we reached the bottom of our coffee cups, I was finding that I had a lot for which to be thankful.

When you see value in something, you invest in it with time, effort, and resources. For the next year, I spent every spare dime on my attitude. As soon as I got paid for my janitorial work, I'd go to the bookstore to buy the latest on attitude. On a good week, I earned close to $225, of which I would spend $25 to $50 on my attitude. Let's just say that I wasn't cheap when it came to my attitude. When you see value in something, you invest in it. Instead of going to the movies, or buying lottery tickets, I invested in books, audios, and seminars. There was a shift in my perspective and a change in my actions. I no longer saw the value in sleeping on the floor, living broke, making excuses, skimming by, and playing the lottery to get back in the game of life. I had a new perspective. The more value I brought to my attitude, the more value my life would experience. My dreams, ambitions, and desire to make a difference, sleep on an actual bed, and have money in my pockets became attainable as I let go of my old habits. My high school basketball coach always said, "You get out of something what you put into it."

I wanted more for my life, so I was like the farmer who goes into the field to plant seeds. I sowed the seeds. I have to tell you, the work was hard, but the harvest made it all worth it.

How about you? What's your story? Where are you right now and where would you like to go?

What does your current attitude say about you?

Is your attitude working for you or against you?

Would an attitude adjustment make things better?

If someone stole your attitude, would it be a blessing?

You get the idea. What is the current state of your attitude? Knowing the value of your attitude is having attitude awareness. If you have a bank account, you want to be aware of what's in the account, what goes out, and what goes in, right? Your attitude is an asset, so the key is to treat it as such. These are some of the questions you have to ask yourself to get and keep your attitude on a positive track.

If You Want Life to Get Better, the Starting Point Is with Your Attitude

We all know what we need to do to get better. We just have to do it! When I got serious about my attitude and took action, the picture of my life began to change. I began to see opportunities where I once saw no exit. As a result, my life began to take a new shape.

If it can happen for a nighttime cleanup guy like me, it can happen to you. I know because I get hundreds of e-mails every year from people telling me their stories. It's a choice you make every day and no one can make it except you.

To cement that concept, last year we started a movement within the Everything Attitude Organization called Attitude Works. Those who choose to participate in this movement sign a declaration stating that they believe "attitude works" in all areas of their lives: relationships, health, finances, a tough economy, and so on. Let me bottom line it: Attitude Works means you believe it works and you take the action to make it work! If you want to participate in this movement, visit our web site, Everything-Attitude.com, and join. It will add value to whatever your cause might be. If you work for a nonprofit, bring the movement Attitude Works to your cause. I am sure attitude plays a vital role in your organization achieving its mission and making a difference. In fact, I would bet your cause starts first with attitude.

What will happen if you begin to value your attitude?

The picture of your life changes.

Attitude Kicker

Why the Right Attitude in Action Can Change Your Life

The right attitude in action is positive energy working for "TEAM You."

What would it be worth to your life, work, relationships, health, and business to experience the following results of the right attitude put into action?

1. You have more motivation to achieve your goals and accomplish things.
2. You expect good things to happen.

3. Problems are opportunities to learn and become better.
4. You have excellent self-esteem because you believe in yourself and your abilities.
5. Your vision improves—you see opportunities in obstacles.
6. You are a more innovative and creative thinker.
7. You are happier and less stressed.
8. You sleep better at night.
9. Your health and heart are in better shape.
10. You have a stronger immune system and are sick less often.
11. You live a longer life.
12. You enjoy having more friends, contacts, and acquaintances because people are attracted to you.
13. You are better able to influence others.
14. You enjoy more respect from others.
15. You lead better and are positively contagious.
16. Your significant other and children like being around you more.
17. Achieving success becomes a lot more fun.
18. Since you expect things will turn out well, you have more perseverance.

Question: Does it cost anything to experience the real benefits of a better attitude? The only cost involved is what are you willing and ready to do to generate all that you want from your attitude. The expense is minimal and simple. The rewards are enormous and go on and on. So give it a try and see what happens.

To stay positively charged, I wish it were as simple as just saying, "*Be positive*," and POOF—it would be done for you and me. If that did work, I would be out of business. The reason that doesn't work is that it lacks action. You can talk about a positive attitude, think about it, write about it, but until you do something about it, it can't happen.

To keep your attitude stuck on positive requires work, or what I like to call "sticking power." You want your efforts to stick. There is action involved, but it carries a reward. If you create just a slight edge of awareness, as Jeff Olsen, author of *The Slight Edge*, says, to how your attitude works and how to put it into action to achieve the results you want, I think you will be amazed at how much the quality of your life, work, and relationships will improve.

You need to also understand that attitude exceeds the definition of simply being positive or negative. There is an anatomy to your attitude. Later, I bring the topic to life for you by showing you the different faces to your attitude, and how you can make each one of them work wonders. You're going to uncover the subtle ways your attitude can work for or against you; and you will see the big changes this can make in your life.

I wasn't thankful for my challenging situations years ago at the time I was experiencing them. I don't think any of us appreciate the hard times we're enduring *while* we're enduring them. But these challenges did more than become the key to my success; they also put me in a classroom that taught me what I am about to share with you. That's the gift I was given.

How is it a gift? Had I not found the opportunity in my setback, I would not be doing what I am doing today, inspiring millions through books, radio, and television on the value of attitude in life. The way I responded to my obstacles then is what has qualified me to impart the insights to which you are about to be introduced.

I am not going to portray myself to be more than who I am in this book or someone I am not. I have had a lot of awesome people play a role in who Sam Glenn, The Attitude Guy, is. I give all my great teachers praise and credit, whether mentioned in this book or not. And I thank you for sharing your greatness. It has changed my life for the better and equipped me to do the same for others.

Attitude in Action

It is not enough to believe that Attitude Works. You have to actively make it work. You and your attitude are partners in life. You can't make attitude work for you if you are in a tug of war or broken down.

What is one action you can take today to declare that Attitude Works?

Declare that Attitude Works in your life! Visit Every-thingAttitude.com to join the movement.

3

A Kick in the Attitude Principle #1

Everything Starts with Your Attitude

Attitude isn't everything, but it is the main thing that affects everything.

—John Maxwell,
Author, *12 Irrefutable Laws of Leadership*

In a study of 3,000 top achievers, researchers found that 85 percent of the subjects attributed their success to their attitude. The other 15 percent attributed their success to their aptitude.

Fifteen percent said their skills provided their success. But let's explore why an overwhelming 85 percent indicated that attitude was so crucial. Let's say you interview 100 sales reps, and the few you hire are going to sell a product you invented. The amount they sell will determine whether you make money. Who would you hire? What traits would you look for in a salesperson?

Suppose you have an applicant with extensive experience, talent, and skills, yet she is known for harboring a negative attitude and not getting along with coworkers. You have another applicant who has slightly fewer skills, but is recognized for displaying a dynamic attitude. She gets along with others very well. Who will you hire?

The editor of my magazine, *Attitude Digest*, recently interviewed a prominent CEO who told the story of a goofy-looking salesperson who was trying to get a job at his company. The fellow didn't have an impressive resume, but he had an amazing attitude. He insisted he was the best man for the job and offered to work for a month for free until things ramped up. Even more, he said that at the end of that period, if the CEO was not convinced of his value, he could let him go, no questions asked. It was an offer too good to refuse, so the CEO's reluctance faded. The outcome of this decision was that the man became the company's best salesperson ever, and was eventually promoted.

Yes, skills are a must, and mixed with the right attitude, you can become a superstar. Yet understand this key point: It's your attitude functioning *through* your skills that will determine whether you fly or fall. If you have the right attitude, you have the necessary edge to get promoted, noticed, and acknowledged. If you have the same set of skills that 100 other people have, the one facet that will separate you from the crowd is the right attitude.

The distinction that will separate the ducks from the eagles is attitude. An eagle will be more open-minded to learning the necessary skills, and possess an attitude that will bring about superior end results.

This formula applies to any occupation or level of employment, from CEOs to administrators, managers, teachers, preachers, assembly line workers, and even athletes. You may be the very best at what you do, with no one able to duplicate your skills, but if you have the wrong attitude, you are as effective as a tornado. Eventually, there will be *negative* consequences. You will make your company and yourself look bad. You will leave bad impressions. You will hurt your relationships. People will complain about you. The picture will only get darker.

Consider an even more compelling angle from which to see how crucial a role your attitude plays in your life. When people have cancer, they first make their personal decisions regarding treatment to combat the disease. Much of the medical community agrees that radiation and medication can sometimes only take a patient so far. The rest may be greatly affected by the individual's attitude.

A study at University of California involving actors showed that they could actually affect their immune systems through the emotions they portrayed. Imagine that: Simply *acting out* an emotion may affect your physicality! Major universities have been studying the effects of mindset and attitude on health, publishing convincing results.

On a personal level, I have spoken with cancer survivors who all tell me that they believe their attitude played a colossal role in their recoveries. They feel that they would not be here if their attitudes had not pulled them through. To me, that speaks volumes.

You might still argue, "What about those who didn't survive, yet had a positive attitude?" Personally, I believe that is a thought for another book, and involves some personal views about life and God. However, it goes without saying that regardless of some things beyond our control, a healthy attitude will serve you better (and make life fuller) than a negative attitude ever will. You do the math.

Chew on This

The power of attitude is that everything of real value to you starts with your attitude.

Success—starts with attitude.

Improvement—starts with attitude.

Getting new business—starts with attitude.

Better customer service—starts with attitude.

Winning—starts with attitude.

A better relationship—

Earning more money—

Losing weight—

Getting the sale—

Getting hired—

All start with attitude.

Now, fill in what *you* are currently facing.

- _____ starts with attitude!
- _____ starts with attitude!
- _____ starts with attitude!

So Why Get a Better Attitude?

The right attitude put into action can help you achieve the following results:

- Sell more—lots more
- Keep clients and attract new ones
- Improve personal relationships
- Attract new opportunities

- Overcome obstacles and setbacks
- Get up, moving, and grooving
- Get hired and promoted
- Become driven to achieve goals
- Make someone's day
- Be more innovative and creative
- Win!
- Live longer and healthier
- Be more attractive!
- Get along better with others

What Is Attitude?

Webster's dictionary defines attitude as a state of emotional being or mindset. More clearly, our attitude is the emotional response we have toward situations and people. It is the mental tone we emit. It is an outward expression of our thoughts and feelings. It is our state of being.

Where Does Our Attitude Come From?

Our attitude is a creation of our thoughts and feelings. These thoughts and feelings can derive from many sources. They may come from our past experiences. They may be shaped by the stimuli we surround ourselves with: family, coworkers, or friends. They may come from what we listen to, watch on television, and read. Combined, we have many elements contributing to the thoughts and feelings, all of which determine the form our attitude will take at a given time. Whatever feeds your mind and emotions also feeds *your attitude*.

First Step: Make Your Attitude Work for You

Jillian Michaels, strength trainer and life coach for NBC's series *The Biggest Loser*, believes you can change your life by changing your mind because the mind directs and drives everything a person does. She tells those she coaches that they must train their minds as intensely as they train their bodies through performing mental exercises to replace self-defeating behaviors with positive ones, as well as remove distractions to bring clarity and self-control.

Our Attitude Is Tested and Challenged Daily

The author John Homer Miller once said, "Your living is determined not so much by what life brings to you, as by the attitude you bring life."

To deepen this point, realize that our attitude is going to be tested daily and how we respond will originate with how we are thinking.

What Determines Our State of Being, or Mindset?

An elderly couple pulled into a full service gas station. The attendant asked the gentleman driver if he wanted the windshield washed. "Certainly," he replied.

The elderly man looked at the window after it was washed and thought, "It's still pretty dirty. I am going to ask him to wash it again."

At that moment, the wife reached over and grabbed the eyeglasses off her husband's face, wiped them clean, and placed them back on his face, resulting in the husband eventually saying, "Those windows look great!"

Attitude is your state of mind, or that looking glass through which you see the world. If the glass is dirty, you will interpret everything accordingly.

Our present thoughts heavily determine our state of being. The way we feel in a given moment can determine our attitude. For example, if we are hungry, stressed, or tired, our attitude is more vulnerable to becoming distracted or turning negative.

However, we are not victims of these outside stressors. We do have options in how we react. In fact, how we interpret situations in our lives determines our mindset; and as we've discovered, our mindset determines our attitude. It is the way in which we *see* the glass.

Dr. Harold Koenig, a prominent psychiatrist and researcher from Duke University and founder of the Center for Spirituality, Theology and Health, recently stated for *Attitude Digest* magazine that while we are born with a certain propensity toward a positive or negative attitude, we have the opportunity to develop skills and mechanisms by which to improve our attitude.

As I mentioned earlier, life will only give you the raw data or information. What you do with it as you work it over in your mind and filter it through your attitude will determine your responses.

Consider this. Everything that happened to you today was in the form of raw data. If you got a flat tire, that would be an example of raw data. If you were fired from your job, that would be raw data. If you found out you won a million dollars, that would be raw data. If someone surprised you with flowers, that would also be raw data.

Your state of mind determines how you interpret this data. It will be filtered through either a negative frame of mind or a positive one. That process, in turn, will determine how your life unfolds.

A kick butt attitude is like a breath of fresh air that will attract opportunities. A sour attitude is like bad breath that can clear a room in a heartbeat, repelling opportunities. Which best describes your current attitude?

Nobody can choose your attitude except you. How we each utilize it is different, but it works the same way for everyone. If it's bad, your life will become more and more empty. If it's good, your life will be full, but it takes work.

Attitude Vultures

Here are 10 attitude "vultures" (vicious hungry birds that want to devour your life) to be aware of, many of which I discuss more throughout the upcoming chapters:

1. Anger
2. Laziness
3. Fear
4. Self-doubt
5. Inflexibility
6. Misplaced priorities
7. Oppressing your "fun factor"
8. Defensiveness

9. Judging others

10. Hatred

Get to Know Your Attitude

Developing a kick butt attitude is a daily process, not a one-day process. Transformation happens with consistency, and so does our success or failure.

You might already have a dynamic attitude, and that's great! The wisdom I am sharing will serve as more wood for the fire.

Attitude in Action

1. What attitude vultures are preying on your attitude today?
2. What one action can you take today to improve the quality of your life?

For the next seven days, define one thing you can do every day to improve the quality of your life. (Turn off the TV, read two pages in a book, eat something healthy, stop complaining for the day, go for a walk, call someone and offer encouragement). You know what you can do to improve your life, and you will learn more about this throughout the book. Doing this will build positive momentum into your attitude.

4

A Kick in the Attitude Principle #2

Transform Your Attitude in the Same Time It Takes to Shower

In essence, if we want to direct our lives, we must take control of our consistent actions. It's not what we do once in a while that shapes our lives, but what we do consistently.

—Tony Robbins,
author of *Awaken the Giant Within*

The Attitude Shower Concept

Have you ever thought about how valuable a shower really is in your life? It's something you (hopefully) do a few minutes every day, but it affects your life in multiple ways.

Question: What if you didn't take a shower or bathe for the next 365 days?

Really think about it.

Okay, now let me ask you:

If you didn't take a shower for the next year, would that affect the way you feel about yourself (confidence, self-image)?

If you didn't bathe for the next year, would it affect your health in a negative way?

Would it affect your love life at all?

How about your job? Or your relationships with co-workers or potential clients and current clients?

Finally, do you think it would eventually affect your finances? I'm pretty sure you would either be let go or would really struggle to find work outside of a smelly basement.

Now, I'm sure the idea of neglecting something so essential feels ridiculous to consider, but just as you allot time in your day for this simple automatic behavior, you have the ability to create time for another priority that will give you a greater quality of life.

How long does it take you to shower every day?

Sam's shower time: *5 to 10 minutes.*

What if you took the same amount of time it takes you to shower to work on your attitude?

This is what I call The Shower Concept. If you dedicate five to ten minutes a day to working on your attitude, you will have results. They might be improved health, stronger finances, better connection with your spouse or kids, or achieving a long-desired dream. Who knows what will spout up from an attitude that has been recharged with life?

To put this another way, would you play an instrument before tuning it? If it was out of tune, would you continue to blare away out of tune? No, you'd instead adjust the instrument until it played optimally.

Some of our lives are completely out of tune, and some of us are only spouting a flat note here and there. Regardless of the current tune of our lives, small attitude adjustments made daily *will* make a cumulative difference in the quality of our lives and keep us playing optimally.

So, like the farmer who goes out to plant seeds, work the field, and reap the harvest, if you want to get something new out of yourself, do what I recommend. It's simple, quick, and easy, so you shouldn't have a problem making it happen.

Do this. Employ the shower concept. This is how you put attitude into action and achieve the results you want.

Attitude Kicker

Do you take 10 minutes to shower? Then read about attitude for ten minutes per day. Here's a simple game plan you can implement.

Read:
4 pages a day for
5 minutes per day
For the next 30 days.
Think you can do this?
YES. YOU CAN!
See if you notice a difference in your life.

If you read four pages a day, five minutes a day, for the next 30 days, you will begin to experience a more energized attitude, a deeper connection to your potential and surge of creativity. Your words will become filled with life, your actions will turn positive, your energy level will increase, and research has also proven that people with better attitudes are more attractive. Need a makeover? Start here!

Attitude in Action

I, _____, am ready to recharge my attitude with the power of a positive kick. For the next 30 days, I will spend as much time making this priority a habit as I do taking a shower, and will read at least four pages of positive material for at least five minutes a day. I will find positive quotes, stories, articles, or books that provide positive energy for my attitude.

Start Date: _____

5

A Kick in the Attitude Principle #3

The Gateway to a Better Attitude Starts the Moment You Lighten Up!

The human race has only one really effective weapon, and that's laughter. The moment it arises, all of hardnesses yield, all our irritations and resentments slip away, and the sunny spirit takes their place.

—Mark Twain

A man appears before St. Peter at the pearly gates. "Have you ever done anything of particular merit?" St. Peter asks.

"Well, I can think of one thing," the man offers. "On a trip to the Black Hills, out in South Dakota, I came upon a gang of macho bikers who were threatening a young woman. I directed them to leave her alone, but they wouldn't listen. So I approached the largest and most heavily tattooed biker. I smacked him on the head, kicked his bike over, ripped out his nose ring and threw it on the ground, and told him, 'Leave her alone now or you'll answer to me.'"

St. Peter was impressed and asked, "When did this happen?"

"Just a couple minutes ago," replied the man.

I love jokes like this. If there is one attitude trait that makes life worth living, it's having a sense of humor. Let me ask you, do you know anyone really uptight? Do you see it as a quality that enriches that person's life or hurts it?

The answer is obvious. I think a lot of people, honestly, are just way too wound up and miss the value of humor and its benefits. The bottom line is we need to lighten up and laugh.

What Does It Mean to Lighten Up?

It means choosing to look at the lighter side of a situation. It's a healthy perspective in which we view the humor around us, enjoying and even celebrating it with others. Humor is like a muscle; in order for it to be effective, it has to be worked out.

Four Reasons to Lighten Up and Laugh It Up

1. Humor has power-packed health benefits

Humor has the health-promoting power to create wellness in your life. When you laugh or have a lighter mood, the body releases endorphins into your system. Endorphins are a group of chemicals that reduce pain, improve sleep, increase the quality of moods, and heal.

The alternate happens when you let tension build. When your body suppresses negative emotions, you are at higher risk for illness, anxiety, depression, mood swings, anger, and frustration. When you allow yourself to live in a state that has limited "humor activity," you can actually age more quickly and become less attractive. We don't even need validation for why we wouldn't want that. Envision someone who is really uptight versus someone who is laughing, enjoying good humor, and smiling. Who might you say appears to have more appeal? Hands down, the person who is using his humor attitude wins.

Another benefit to having a good sense of humor is that it will give you the coping power to deal with whatever life throws your way. It does not mean that you avoid negative emotions. It means that your body and mind will help you respond more favorably in order to combat your thoughts and moods with emotions such as hope, joy, love, optimism, and caring.

According to Dr. Bill Fry at Stanford University, laughing 200 times burns off the same amount of calories as 10 minutes on a rowing machine. Laughter oxygenates your blood, increases energy, and relaxes your muscles. Studies show that laughter also strengthens your immune system.

Many hospitals today are incorporating what is known as "laugh therapy" or "humor programs." The purpose is to help speed a recovery. Do you remember the movie *Patch Adams*, and how he used humor to lift people's spirits? Patch felt that it was a necessary part of healing. Today, hospital beds are filled with people who have stress-related illnesses, meaning they could get up and go *physically, but mentally they need inspiration.*

In 1964, Norman Cousins—political journalist, author, professor, and peace activist—was diagnosed with a debilitating disease called ankylosing spondylitis, a form of arthritis. His physicians gave him little hope for recovery. Norman read a book by psychologist Hans Selye about how the body responds to stress. It described how negative emotions could create chemical changes that would lead to exhaustion. He suspected that the positive emotions such as faith, hope, and joy might create changes within the body that might enhance the recovery process. Since the behavior of laughter opens the door to these positive emotions, Cousins began to watch funny movies to stimulate laughter. He noticed that after each episode, he would sleep better and need less medication. His body began to heal, and the medical community took notice. I especially love the story about how he took his apple juice and poured it into the cup used to take urine samples. The nurse walked in, saw the cup and color of its contents, and said, "Norman, this does not look right."

Norman grabbed the cup from her and said, "You are right, I guess I better run it through again." And he drank it. The nurse just about passed out! Norman just laughed!

2. You are your best source for humor

If we simply choose to lighten up and look around and at ourselves, we will discover an abundance of humor. The sign of a healthy attitude is when we can laugh at ourselves. Our ability to laugh is our gift from God. When we act on that ability, we internalize that gift. When we spread laughter to others, we shower others with gifts.

Over the years, I have had to learn to see the humor around and in myself, which can be tough, as not everything is funny when it first happens. The more you practice humor, the easier it is to laugh when things go wrong.

And things do go wrong. Years ago, I was a guest at a friend's house. I went to brush my teeth and realized I had forgotten my toothpaste. But it was okay. I noticed a tube on the counter. I loaded up my toothbrush and began to brush, but noticed it did not have a minty-fresh taste. I picked up the tube to read what kind of strange toothpaste these people were using. To my surprise, it read Preparation H! Instead of getting angry, I activated my humor attitude and laughed.

The list just adds up for me. I have walked through the Atlanta airport with a very long piece of toilet paper trailing off the back of my pants, fallen down an escalator, gotten my leg stuck in a revolving door, and walked into a glass door like a bug hitting a windshield. While none of these experiences were funny to me right away, I was able—through my practice of lightening up and looking for the humor—to find the joy in each situation. I can now look back at any of these moments, think about the scenarios, and have a good laugh. That's the power of choosing to see the lighter side of events. You can reflect on them at any time and embrace the rewards.

A healthy attitude exists when we can laugh at ourselves and the crazy things we do, or find humor in what happens to us on a daily basis. It takes some practice, but is so worth it. Make humor a healthy habit and attitude in your life. The benefits: You will feel good and look good!

3. Humor can help you become more successful

Think about Ronald Reagan. When he passed on and people acknowledged him, every person recognized two things about him—his leadership and his humor. His humor made him likeable. It broke the ice at meetings. It made people feel comfortable and eased the tension of stressful situations.

You don't have to be a comedian to incorporate good humor. Just choose to see the lighter side in situations and yourself. That's what Reagan did, and it added to his success.

Thomas Edison is praised for all his great inventions, but one of his greatest discoveries was in recognizing humor's effect on life and work. Edison had notebooks and notebooks filled with humor and jokes. He collected humor material and shared it constantly with his staff and family. He discovered that a staff that laughs together works harder and more effectively together.

If you interview any successful leader, I bet that he or she will tell you that having a sense of humor is vital to great leadership. It keeps things in perspective.

4. Humor can save you from terminal professionalism

Do you work with people who might have a little terminal professionalism? They may be uptight, negative, and not enjoyable to be around. Are you like this at all? Here is a good way to test yourself: If you walk out of a room and hear celebrations or people praising God behind you, consider it a sign you need to lighten up.

It's understandable that we have a lot on our plates at work and carry hefty responsibilities. Frustration can build when others are not working well with us. There's no doubt that the workplace has become a factory for burnout and stress-related illnesses. There are so many factors that cause stress: deadlines, difficult people, sitting in traffic, phones ringing and the list goes on.

Did you know that more people drop dead on Monday before work than any other day of the week? It's safe to say, people are dying not to go to work. If you don't enjoy what you do, it can make you uptight and negative.

So what can you do? As we've discussed, you may not be able to control what's going on at work and what's going on around you, but you do have the power to choose how you respond to what's going on. Remember, your perception determines your responses.

Keeping your sense of humor will help you respond in healthy ways. It will relax you. You will breathe better and enjoy your work more. Humor is to your life as what shocks are to a car. It helps you endure the bumps along the way.

Companies are recognizing the importance of wellness programs that incorporate mental components like humor. If the workplace is creating suppressed negativity, people will become unhealthy. Productivity will drop, creativity will decrease, service will be out to lunch all day, and teamwork will be sleeping on the couch in the break room. It is of value to the company and its future to keep morale up. Bottom line: When we feel good, we do well, and everyone wins.

Using Humor in the Workplace

Janice Fields, COO of McDonald's, says, "Laugh a lot. . . . Whatever behaviors the boss has, people tend to emulate."

Dr. Joel Goodman, author of *Laffirmations: 1,001 Ways to Add Humor to Your Life and Work*, and director of The Humor Project, wrote the following on www.thehumorproject.com: "The funny line and the bottom line intersect as a survey of 737 CEOs was done and 98% of them said they would much rather hire somebody with a good sense of humor versus someone who has a glum outlook on life. You can take your job seriously, but yourself lightly." (Survey, Hodge Cronin and Associates)

Employ Humor in the Workplace

Here are the benefits of using humor in the workplace:

- Humor creates positive human connection.
- Humor can lighten up meetings.

- Humor creates an attitude that makes you more likeable.
- Humor causes people to enjoy what they do more.
- Humor can open the door to a prospective client.
- Humor can help you become more resilient in challenging situations.
- People who have a good sense of humor are more self-confident.

Ken Blanchard, author of the best-selling *One-Minute Manager*, says, "Humor and laughter in organizations can increase the amount of feedback you can get, the honesty, and the capacity for people to tell you good things. All the solutions to problems in organizations are within your own people, but the problem is half of them don't want to say anything, because they usually get zapped—you kill the messenger. It's through humor that you *can* open up the lines to communication."

Companies that cultivate humor in the workplace also cultivate people who will serve better, feel better, and work better. Some of us do need to lighten up, and the way we do that is by choosing to look on the lighter side of situations.

Attitude Kicker

HERE IS A STORY YOU MIGHT LIKE . . .

Two elderly women were sitting on a bench waiting for a bus. The buses were running late, and a lot of time passed. Finally, one woman turned to the other and said, "You know, I've been sitting here so long, my butt fell asleep."

The other woman turned to her and said, "I know, I heard it snoring."

Remember . . . *Humor is all around us.* As you practice the steps I described, you will begin to see more and more things that will lighten you up and have you laughing out loud.

Humorous One-Liners from Comedian Steven Wright

1. "If it's true that we are here to help others, then what exactly are others here for?"
2. "If FedEx and UPS were to merge, would they call it FED UP?
3. What hair color do they put on a driver's license of a bald man?"
4. "If lawyers are disbarred and clergymen defrocked, doesn't it follow that electricians can be delighted, musicians denoted, cowboys deranged, models deposed, tree surgeons debarked, and dry cleaners depressed?"

Funny Newspaper Ads

NORDIC TRACK
$300 hardly used, call Chubby.
WEDDING DRESS FOR SALE
Worn once by mistake.
Call Stephanie.
SET OF ENCYCLOPEDIAS FOR SALE
Just got married, wife knows it all.
JOINING A NUDIST COLONY
Washer and Dryer for Sale.

GEORGIA PEACHES
California Grown - 89 cents/lb.
FREE YORKSHIRE TERRIER
8 Years Old. Hateful Little Dog. Bites.
WEDDING RING FOR TRADE
Need a Hand Gun.

Four Quick Ways to Activate Your Humor Muscle

1. **First, make the choice to lighten up.**

   Give yourself permission to enjoy something funny. If you're not enjoying humor around you, you need to ask yourself, *why not?* What limitation have you created in your mind that is serving as a roadblock to enjoying the lighter side of life? I gotta tell you, you're missing out. Are you blaming something or someone? Figure it out, and once you do, get over it—and fast. Hey! It's okay to have a good chuckle. Who cares if you look weird laughing and others see you?

   I am not saying you should laugh at everything. Learn to laugh at the pure, the positive, and the good. Don't laugh at the expense of others. Don't laugh at things that are distasteful. Laugh at effective and healthy humor.

2. **Practice.**

   Humor is a muscle; if you don't work it out, it can't work for you. You don't have to be a comedian to experience or communicate good humor; just choose to see the lighter side of situations and yourself. That's the starting point. Start off small, then gradually you will begin to see and experience more humor in your life.

3. **Stay around people who laugh.**

Laughter is contagious. It's always fun to be around someone who loves to laugh. Sooner rather than later, you will join in.

4. **Collect humorous material.**

Rent a funny movie and have a belly laugh. I like to cut out funny cartoons and post them for all to see. My personal favorite humor-gathering activity is collecting humorous stories and sharing them. That's part of why I started *Attitude Digest* magazine, so people could take a break from all the stress at work, and laugh a little, while they also learn some great tips.

Attitude in Action

Are you uptight? Or do you know how to lighten up and enjoy the humor that surrounds you?

Action: Collect something funny this week. Pause for a moment and see if you can notice something funny around you and then laugh about it. Practice this over and over until you get it.

A Kick in the Attitude Principle #4

Attitude Nourishment—A Small Dose of Vitamin A Can Turn a Dull, Negative Person Positive

Take a white board, some colored markers, and the most negative office in the world—add a positive quote every day, and something cool begins to happen. . . .

Before I graduated from college, I applied for an internship with a very large firm that happened to be ranked number one in its industry. Everyone I majored with hoped to work there. I remember thinking, *if they are number one, this must be the best company to work for. It must be comprised of the most positive, dynamic people in the world.*

I was wrong. There were so many negative, rude, and depressing people at the company that I began to think that whole number one thing must have been a clerical error. It was actually quite shocking. There were times when I wondered how certain people around me had even been hired. After being there a few weeks, I was becoming just like my environment. I was starting to get rude, negative, and depressed. I wanted to quit; I stuck it out, though, thanks in part to an inspirational calendar my mom gave me as a gift. There were motivational words on each day of the week. I would read and repeat them to myself all day long just to get through the day.

Eventually, something happened that was so incredible it literally changed my life. My mom had given me that calendar with the expectation it would have a positive impact on my attitude. But when you are focusing on the negative, you never think that something seemingly "small" like this has the potential to change the situation. Watch out! Something good *does* soak in, and it begins to push the bad stuff out. Your thinking changes, your responses are altered, your attitude improves, and then your world is transformed. That's when you realize that attitude's impact is more than mumbo jumbo.

That's exactly what happened to me. Slowly, the positive words began to sink in and change the way I saw things. I was actually starting to look forward to the quotes, and was looking for the good around me, instead of focusing so much on what was wrong. Everything was changing; and it was for the better. I had previously been letting my emotions determine my behavior. Without even realizing it, my behavior—the words I read and repeated, and the way I moved my body—changed and influenced my emotions. I found a rhythm in my step, a smile on my face, and a kick in my attitude. I took it a step further. I thought: If those words can change me, perhaps they can change others around me in the workplace.

I took some initiative and attempted something that was somewhat risky, but could, I hoped, change the work environment. Right near my desk, there was a huge white board that was hardly used. One day, I took some colored markers and wrote some inspirational quotes up there—nice and big for all to see. The response was amazing. Everyone—and I do mean *everyone*—stopped to read them. The quotes would either put a smile on their faces, or a look that said, "Hmmm, let me think more about that. That's good stuff."

One VP who stopped by was so inspired by the quote of the day that he would make sure that a new one would be up every day. He'd say, "I'll be back for the new quote tomorrow," to which I would reply, "I'll be looking for you!"

When I left that internship, the staff had a nice send-off party for me. My coworkers talked about how my attitude had touched their lives and made bad days better, how it had gotten them to focus more clearly on life and what they were doing.

I had started where I was, and used attitude to make a difference. I believed that it would work, and spent a few minutes every day not only nurturing my attitude, but also changing my environment. I decided to create an input of great material. The result was that the cumulative actions and attitude of personnel improved. Can you do something like this today, despite your circumstances? *Absolutely!*

Attitude Kicker:

Even the smallest positive input can change a negative environment.

The Vitamin A Concept

You take daily vitamins, right? If you don't, you at least likely try to eat well enough to ensure you get the most crucial vitamins so that your teeth don't fall out. Do the same thing with your attitude. Nurture it every day with something small. This is a way to start your day, and it is a way you can start your attitude recharge. It's something small that makes a big difference. Here are three small ways to start employing The Vitamin Concept:

1. Read inspirational quotes every day. Start your day off with breakfast and a quote. To make it easier, you can purchase a book of quotes. I have one called *Attitude Kickers*, compiled by readers and fans who have sent me their favorites collected over the years (see Everything-Attitude.com).

2. Jot down a few positive things every day. This can be a short list of what you are thankful for, or perhaps something good that happened to you.

3. Pass these vitamins along to others as well. Send your favorite quotes or motivational stories to those who need them most.

Attitude in Action

What can you do today, in the amount of time it takes you to eat a vitamin, to nurture your attitude?

Define three things that will be your Vitamin A (your source for developing a positive attitude in the same amount of time it takes you to eat a vitamin).

7

A Kick in the Attitude Principle #5

Your Attitude Is Either in the Way, On the Way, or Creating a Way

Life is about managing the things that we tolerate. What are you no longer willing to tolerate? What is currently bad enough for your life that you are willing to let it go?

Once I was on an airplane flight, with an overtired mind, and I kept dwelling on a negative thought, watching it spiral and grow in my imagination. Eventually, I started turning red with anger while sitting in my seat. I would have kept on that path of thinking for another hour—and my day would have been ruined—had it not been for a big old cloud that shook our plane.

When that plane hit turbulence, was I still thinking about my negative thought? Not at all. My pattern was broken, and my thinking interrupted. I had a new thought: wondering when the plane would stop jumping around!

When the turbulence was over, I had a choice: I could either go back to thinking the bad thoughts that didn't benefit me in any way; or I could let the whole issue go and think about something that lifted my spirits. I had enough awareness of my thoughts that I could see the choice clearly, so I let my troubles go and built my day on a more productive outlook. All thanks to a nice jolt!

Whether you are dwelling on a little problem or zapped by the shock of turbulence, the lesson is the same: Get over it and get on with it! That's my philosophy when it comes to the obstacles in life that get in the way of achieving greatness or being our best. When I say get on with it, I am referring to moving to a place where you are not hung up, caught up, or tripped up by your self-inflicted limitations, but are instead moving on and getting the best out of life and yourself. It takes courage and humility to take this step, but it is well within your power to do so.

Are you aware of something that is keeping you hung up or distanced from where you want to be in life? Is something blocking you from achieving your dreams and happiness? Is this thing keeping you from having fulfilling and connected relationships? What's in the way? Is it perhaps not an "it"—but rather a "who"?

Attitude Kicker

What would the picture of your life look like without your self-imposed limitations?

What Is "It" for You? Is It

- Fear?
- Past experience?
- Laziness?

- Someone who hurt you who you can't forgive or forget?
- An excuse of some sort?
- Negative attitude?

Notice that each of these limitations is internal. That's great news, because it means we are in control of the situation, and have the power to change it.

Whatever it is, you need to reframe it into something positive. You need to get over it and on with it if you are ever going to experience life to the fullest, and you need to start looking at the good around you. You can't get to the "more" until you overcome what's in the way of it. This is easier said than done, but the very act of deciding to get over it will put you well on your way. You have raised the bar for your life. You are ready to explore beyond your current boundaries, to see what life really has to offer you. Start by experimenting with letting go of the small problems and you will have better odds against the more major obstacles.

Rose-colored glasses don't work; however, getting an attitude eye examination might not be a bad idea . . .

The process of overcoming limitations doesn't fully begin until you have a willingness to change, improve, and unlock the shackles you have knowingly or unknowingly placed on yourself. To get the best out of life and yourself, you have to get real with yourself and address this question: What negative limitations are keeping you from your best—your best attitude, best choices, best thinking, the best that life has to offer? Identify what is in the way and placing you in a rut, preventing you from getting the promotion, making your relationships stale rather than enriched, keeping you from winning more sales, igniting strife with coworkers, distancing you from a healthy lifestyle. Ask yourself these six questions:

1. Do I complain a lot?
2. Do I have a short temper—does everything seem to get on my nerves?
3. Do I judge others and criticize?
4. Do I believe nothing goes my way and I am always a victim?
5. Am I too controlling?
6. Do I suffer from low self-esteem?

It will be hard to accept new positive concepts and actually see that they work if you are hung up on something and not willing to face, conquer, and move past it. Really, what's occurring here is identity theft, in that something or someone is robbing you of your superstar status in life. And the purpose of knowing what's limiting you is that you will then know exactly what you need to conquer.

Attitude Kicker

Most limitations do not start outside of us; they start on the inside, and work their way out. We create most of our own boundaries. Examine your limitations and work on overcoming them. When you do, the world around you will begin to seem better!

I recently received the following letter from someone who had heard me speak on this topic.

Dear Sam,

I have been trying to encourage a friend now for years. He was abused by his parents and has been seeing counselors with very little progress. He is always depressed. I am not sure what else I can do to encourage him. He is starting to bring me down. It's like he won't let go of the past.

My response:

It's always nice to know that there are people like you who will reach out with a touch of encouragement. Sadly, your friend had an experience that is taking time to get through. Getting over it and on with it may happen in an instant; or may take years. Our attitude plays a big role in that process. Your friend is not ready to let go of the past, and as a result, he can't see what's in front of him. When our attitude is not right, nothing else appears to be right, either. Your friend's limitation is not created by what happened to him, but by his tight hold on the experience, which is allowing it to rule his very existence.

I might suggest giving him some positive examples of people who have gone through similar situations and have emerged victorious. The best example I can give you is a woman who airs her talk show in the city I call home. Her name is Oprah! Also, if your friend reaches out to help others who have battled or are battling the same situation, he will find renewed strength; because what we send out really does come back to us, and multiplied. He may even discover his true calling and purpose.

When bad things happen, we can choose to use them rather than let them use us. The only thing is that in order to turn it all around, we have to pinpoint what's limiting us in order to get over and get on with it. Your friend has to come to a crossroads. He has to decide that his life is worth much more than what he is currently believing or demonstrating. And then he has to start discovering and acting upon his own worth, a little bit at a time, until his life changes—not by accident, but because he is investing in the direction he wants to go. Be encouraging and don't give up. Remember, all encouragement makes a difference.

—Sam Glenn

If You Can't See the Limitation, What Do You Do?

It may not be enough to hold a mirror to our lives, because a lot of the time we may not see anything wrong. Years ago, I wrote a letter to 26 people and proofed the letter 10 times. I thought I got all the spelling and grammar fixed, but to my surprise, my assistant pointed out that I had actually missed something— something big. (And the letter had already been mailed. I had failed to have anyone else look it over before I sent it.) In the letter, I wanted to indicate that I had matured over the years. But what it actually said was, "I have manured over the years." Two vastly different experiences for the reader! I was devastated because I thought, *How could I miss that? That, of all things!*

Even though the mistake was a huge one, I missed it despite having reread my own letter 10 times. The same occurs within our lives. If you have trouble finding the answers on your own, I suggest discussing the issue with someone you know who cares about you, whether that's a friend, family member, or counselor who may offer a unique and valuable perspective.

Seeking the help of others is in no way an act of weakness; rather, it demonstrates your active willingness to get over what's keeping you from getting the best out of life.

Ask this person if he or she sees a limitation in your life that you don't. Talk it out. Be prepared; you may not always like what you hear. Others might tell you something that shocks you, or something you have heard over and over for years but simply ignored. It's also good to ask your friend or family member to point out the good things in you and your life. Positive feedback is also very helpful; it has the power to encourage and validate that not everything about you is negative. It gives you something to work from and to expand on.

The key to making this work for you will lie in your willingness to apply constructive criticism in a positive way. It's not easy by any means.

You may have heard this before . . . Change will happen when the pain of remaining the same is worse than the pain of changing.

Does the limitation standing in your way hurt enough for you to want to change? Consider this story, which has been around for a while. A young man was taking a walk when he noticed a man rocking in a chair on his porch. Next to the man was an old hound dog. Every so often, the dog would yelp. The young man inquired, "Is that dog okay?"

"Sure, he is just lying on a nail," answered the old man.

"Well, why doesn't he move?" asked the young man.

"Guess it doesn't hurt him enough," the old man replied.

Your limitations—no matter how big or how seemingly insignificant—will remain in front of you and affect your life in a negative way until you choose to change your mind and deal with them, get over them, and get on with it. Even those limitations that don't seem like a big deal are still affecting you. So why not get over them, too?

Once you decipher what is getting in your way, it's up to you to summon the courage to *get over it and get on with it*. At some point, you have to be willing to let go of the limitation and conquer it. You have to be willing to change your choices, your perspective, and your attitude. Once you deal with your limitations, you will discover a spring in your step and a kick in your attitude. You will no longer need to yelp over those annoying nails. Instead, you can run around and bark!

Attitude in Action

Define what's in your way.

What would your life look like if you got them out of the way?

What actions do you need to take to get over your limitations?

What needs to change in your life in order for this to happen?

Take a moment, flip to your journal or to the Notes page in the back of the book, and jot down your answers.

A Kick in the Attitude Principle #6

If You Don't Like the Picture of Your Life, Start Painting Something Different

Imagination is everything, it's the preview to life's coming attractions.

—Albert Einstein

Have you ever had a day start when something not so great happened and seemed to mess up your positive vibe? Many people allow whatever bad happens to them during the day to define the rest of the day. Perhaps you've said, "Well, that's how my day will go!"

Joan Lunden was interviewed about her attitude and said the best advice she ever got was that if her day started off bad, she should start it over. I like to say, "The rest of my day will be the best of my day." That simple statement puts a positive expectation in front of me, versus, "Well, it's gonna be a bad day, all day!"

Change your attitude and you will change what you *see* in front of you.

I once had the opportunity to start my day over.

Many years ago, I was invited to speak to 13,000 people about attitude. I had to catch a flight at 6:00 A.M. I had to run to my gate and knocked over a family of 10 (okay, not really, it was just one guy, but everything felt amplified that day).

All they had for me was a middle seat, which, at 6'7", didn't exactly thrill me. When I sat down, it was obvious I didn't fit, and the woman next to me just laughed. As soon as we were in the air, the guy in front of me leaned his chair back. I thought to myself, "You've gotta be kidding." Then the guy next to me kept wanting to have a conversation and had the worst breath ever. I had tears in my eyes. I would say I was in a good position to explode. My attitude went to the dark side. I was hungry, stressed, tired, and ready to wrestle people to the ground.

I had to stop and remind myself, "Attitude is a choice. It's my attitude and it's my choice. What can I do to get back to my best attitude or at least a better one than I have now?"

When I got off the airplane, I got a bottle of water and a bag of pretzels and began talking to myself with empowering words. I began to feel a little better and actually felt my best attitude coming back. But, my attitude was about to face an unexpected challenge.

It Ain't Over Until You and 200 People See Your Underwear

I was feeling back to normal again as I walked to pick up my luggage. I met my sponsor and we chitchatted about the event. It was then that I heard an eruption of laugher. Curious as to what everyone was having such a good time about, I looked around to see somebody's luggage coming around the carousel, with four pairs of underwear taped to the outside. At first, I started wailing in laughter. What better way to change my attitude than a little real life comedy? I was ready to take advantage of the situation!

But then the contraption came closer, and the print on those Fruit of the Looms looked a little too familiar.

"*What the*?!"

Apparently, the top of my luggage had ripped off and the luggage guys had reassembled it by putting the top part on first, my clothes on top of that, and then four pairs of underwear on top of that. I should mention that the tape covering it was the clear type.

I was beside myself trying to figure out what had happened. And to avoid escalating an embarrassing situation, I ignored my bag as it went around 13 times on the carousel. The hoot of is, nobody was leaving. They all wanted to see who owned the bag.

The point is, I changed the picture of the situation. Rather than have a horrible day, I decided I was going to make the best of it, and turn it into something positive. I allowed myself to see the humor, and laughed with the crowd and my sponsor when I finally grabbed my "custom designed" bag. I changed the picture of the moment, and in doing so, changed the picture of my life. I started over, and recreated.

When Your Whole Life Needs a Do-Over

Maybe it is not just your day that has gone badly, but your entire life. You may even be thinking that it's too late to change. You have lived this way for so long, or you have gotten yourself into so much trouble, that there is no way out. Life will never be wonderful for you, you may think, because it would take too much work to get there.

Think about that for a moment. Why would you accept mediocrity, when you have the choice to create excellence? If the picture of your life is ugly right now, and even if it has always been ugly, you can *still* wake up today and decide to change it all.

I know, because I have done it, and because I have heard from so many people who had been sitting in the middle of an ugly life painting, changed their attitudes, and changed their lives.

Actress Hilary Swank changed the picture of her life. She spent her childhood living in a trailer park in Bellingham, Washington. "I had a roof over my head and I had food and I had love, and it was not a big deal," she has said. "But it was at that age that I learned classism, because of my friends—not my friends, but my friends' parents—who wouldn't allow their kids to play with me, like I was somehow contagious and they would all become poor or something." She found relief from her loneliness through acting. When her parents divorced, she and her mother moved to Los Angeles with just $75. Within a year, she was on television, and eventually her career led her to win two Best Actress Oscars. Still, she says, "I don't know what I did in this life to deserve this. I'm just a girl from a trailer park who had a dream."

Painting a new picture starts with your attitude. The amazing thing about acrylic and oil paints is that once they dry, the canvas can be reused. You can repaint an entirely different picture, in the same spot. So it goes with your life . . . You can start today, and change the picture of your attitude and life. The result is a different outlook, experience, result, and feelings. If we can do this daily, our life as a whole will begin to change.

Here are a few tips for painting a positive picture for your life.

1. *Trade blame for responsibility.* You are where you are, have what you have, and are getting what you are getting because of your choices. You were born with your own set of wings. If you are not using them, there is no one else to blame. Even if you *do* have someone to blame for something in your past that knocked you down, you are the one responsible for staying on the ground—if that is where you still are. Once you recognize that you have fallen, you have the option to get up and move on, and the obligation to yourself to act on that option if you want to see change in your life.

   You have to take responsibility for your life; if you don't, who will? Don't blame everything and everyone for your misfortunes. We all face challenges that knock us down; the question is, what are you going to do about them? Are you going to stay down and blame the world, or get up, grow up, and move on? When you stop blaming others and making excuses about why you are living the life that you are, you will gain a new and refreshing perspective on life.

   Unless you are mentally or extremely physically incapable, then you have *no excuses*—not a single one. In fact, even people with some unbelievable physical challenges, like Helen Keller, have overcome tremendous obstacles to reach greatness. If you feel inadequate, it is

---

Attitude Kicker

If we did all the things we are capable of doing, we would literally astound ourselves.

—Thomas Edison

---

because you have allowed the negative thoughts, the past, or something else unsavory to be the master of your destiny. We are not perfect and we do not live in a perfect world. People will hurt us; some will take advantage of us. We will make mistakes and fail; but blaming the government, the weather, our ex-partner, or anything else will not help us achieve our dreams.

Accepting responsibility for your future is one of the greatest steps you can take in drawing closer to your goals. If something goes wrong or things get tough, accept it, live, learn, and climb on. You can either sit on the side of the road and tell shoulda, woulda, coulda stories or you can take ownership of your destiny and get moving.

2. *Be flexible.* We get attached to our own way of doing things, but we need to be open to change—see the lighter side, have fun, and go somewhere new with our attitude.

3. *Let go of your drama.* Sometimes it's easier to hold on to the negative stuff that happens to us, and it provides us with some comfort, especially when it's familiar. Marlene Chism, speaker and founder of the Stop Your Drama methodology, has a concept called "Get in the shade or go

home." Basically, instead of complaining about the heat, we can spend that same energy on stepping aside into the shade. When we let go of our drama, whether it be the past or something going on right now, we free ourselves to see what is out there for us, in a positive way. We become able to reinvent our lives.

Attitude in Action

If you could describe the current picture of your life, what does it look like?

Think for a moment like an artist. What needs to change? What needs a touch-up? What's good as is? What do you need to do in order to paint something new, or overcome something old?

A Kick in the Attitude Principle #7

When You Doubt Yourself, You Defeat Yourself

A positive attitude is a self imposed blessing.
—Jeffrey Gitomer,
"Celebrate Yourself and Create a New Attitude"
Dallas Business Journal, March 30, 2001

In 1990, when I was a senior in high school, I had a real passion for basketball. One night as I sat there humped over my dinner, I could not stop the tears from rolling down my face. I had my heart set on a basketball scholarship. But it seemed like a faint wish at this point that would not come true. I had injured my knee a few months before and the recovery was going slowly. I had just returned home from a basketball practice wherein my coach told me how disappointed he was in me and my performance. I had very little confidence in myself and I could understand my coach's frustration. I was a team leader and my injury was hurting the team. I was not performing up to my previous ability. I sat there at a crossroads and contemplated quitting. I knew giving up would not show leadership, but I just didn't want to sit on the bench.

As I sat there trying to eat what my mom had kept warm for hours, I opened the newspaper. Every other Thursday the area paper would show the statistics of all the top area players—points averaged per game, rebounds, and all that good stuff. After the start of the season, I was at the bottom in almost every category and nonexistent on the rebound list. It was embarrassing. I was a big man averaging less than six rebounds per game. It was my role on the team to get rebounds and I was not living up to that expectation.

I was dead last in the rankings. Instead of wallowing one more minute in my situation, I made up my mind right there that I was going to turn it all around. My goal was to go to the top. It was an outrageous goal, because I was in the company of some incredible players. I knew it would be a tough race and a long shot, but I was at the bottom with only one place to go— *up*. I had nothing to lose by aiming and shooting for the top. I set my heart and my mind to it and, with faith in my abilities, away I went . . .

Let me pause for a moment and tell you that the change in my attitude was my decision to define what I wanted—a goal, a target, a dream (which I discuss more in future chapters). Then, I chose to *believe* I could achieve it.

You will very rarely have or become what you do not believe in. You gain everything when you have confidence in yourself, and lose it all when you doubt yourself. Believing in yourself in a positive way creates an energy that propels you toward your dreams.

You have just got to believe! You have nothing to lose when you do.

For weeks, rebounding was all I could think about. I would see my name being listed as number one on the statistic sheet for

area rebounds. I would visualize myself going after every rebound. My performance turned around dramatically. My body
was following the direction in which my mind was propelling
me. My teammates and coach could not believe the turnaround.

There were still some odds against me. I was rehabilitating
an injured knee. I wore an Omni brace, which is a huge leg brace
that keeps your knee stable, preventing a blowout. While it
protected my knee, it added weight and took time to get used to.

When game time came, I was a maniac. It wasn't long
before I found myself moving toward the picture in my mind.
I was getting 10 rebounds a game, then 15, then 18, and then
22. If that ball came off the rim, I knew it was mine! My hands
became glue. In fact, one of my teammates picked up on what I
was doing and he started going after rebounds like crazy. He
went from averaging 4.5 rebounds to getting 9, 12, and sometimes 15 rebounds a game. My drive and determination raised
the level of my teammates. As I write this I have goose bumps,
because it was so incredible!

Weeks passed into the season and I wasn't sure where I
stood in the ratings. I saw my name on the bottom of the list,
and the middle, but didn't stop believing in reaching the top.
The final Thursday, in which I would see the year-end standings, came. I was nervous on the car ride home from practice.
I want to point out that I didn't tell anyone what I was doing and
believing in—not even my family. My goal was strictly personal.
As I walked in the front door, I could see the paper sitting on the
counter next to my dinner. I felt like Charlie in *Willy Wonka and
the Chocolate Factory*, when he opened up the chocolate bar to
win the golden ticket. I ate a few bites of my dinner and slowly
opened the paper to the standings page. I glanced really quickly
and I didn't even see my name on the list. My heart skipped a
beat and I thought, *This can't be right. I have been averaging so*

many rebounds. I took a deep breath and looked again, and then I realized why I didn't see my name at first. I was looking at the bottom of the list, to make sure I wasn't there, and the middle, because that's where I was when I had last checked. But, when I looked at the very top to see who was the #1 top rebounder, I saw these words: SAM GLENN.

I put the paper down on the counter and started to cry because I had reached my goal. It took so much hard work and determination, but in that moment I tasted what true victory in reaching goals is all about. I honestly wasn't sure if I could do it or not, *but I tried and gave it my very best.* I set my heart and mind to it, envisioning it and acting on it, and it happened— even more perfectly than I would have imagined.

Attitude Kicker

Building confidence in yourself is a daily process. Step by step, you can rebuild, or build it completely from scratch.

It is true. You really can achieve greatness when your heart and mind are fully in it. Tapping your potential starts with believing in yourself.

When You Doubt Yourself, You Defeat Yourself

When you believe in yourself, you have everything to gain and nothing to lose. It's okay to believe in yourself. It's good to believe in yourself. Believing in yourself is not about ego, but rather about confidence. It means knowing you have what it takes to achieve, move forward, and attract what you desire into your life.

Don't Believe the Naysayers

Some people may say some cruel things to you and try to keep you down, but you don't have to believe them. You get to choose what to believe.

Think of it this way. If you had an authentic and rare diamond, what would you think if a group of people came up to you and spouted, "That's not real! It's worth only about $10. It's nothing!" You would know that what they were saying was false, because you have knowledge of its real value!

When you realize who you are and the potential you possess, the same truth will apply. People will often put you down and try to keep you from the prize, but knowing the truth frees you from the lies and even prevents you from considering the negative comments of others.

Give yourself permission to believe in the greatness of who you are, and when you do, incredible things will happen in your life.

Some might not realize that Jim Carrey didn't start his comedy career with success. As a child, he performed constantly for anyone who would watch, and even mailed his resume to *The Carol Burnett Show* when he was 10 years old. Talk about confidence! His adolescence, however, found him working security and janitorial jobs, and living out of a VW camper. His debut into comedy was reportedly awful at standup clubs in Toronto, but he kept going. In 1979, he moved to Los Angeles to pursue his career. After landing on *In Living Color*, he got noticed, and is now one of the highest paid actors, and a Golden Globe winner. What kept him going? Undoubtedly he believed in himself, even when others, or life, didn't. He had enough courage to *try*, over and over again.

Attitude Kicker

Here some truths to embrace and live by: You are a person of worth and value and nobody can take that away from you. Once you believe that and embrace it in your mind and body, your confidence will build and the results can be seen.

Five steps to building personal confidence

1. *Affirm it with words.* Use language not only to reinforce who you are, but to reinforce whatever it is that you want to achieve. Writing professors often tell students to call themselves writers, even before they are selling novels. Say "when" I get such and such promotion, rather than "if." This helps you build confidence in your dreams, and in yourself. You also never know who you might attract into your life to help your dreams come true, if you are using the right language. Confidence sells *you*.

2. *Think it.* Believe the words you speak about yourself. Visualize your success. Truly accept that you are a wonderful, unique person who has something special to offer.

3. *Do something easy first.* If you can't tackle the huge project out of the gate, set a small goal for yourself. Do something you are good at. If you can accomplish your realistic short-term goals, you'll gain knowledge and confidence to tackle something more lofty next.

4. *Practice.* I've seen a lot of people who avoid what they are bad at, and it keeps eating at them. If you are crummy at sales, but want and need to be good at it, practice it 10 times more than anything else, until it becomes second nature. Let that hope and confidence feed your courage, until your skills become strong enough to help you soar.

5. *Fake it.* If you still struggle with having confidence in your abilities or future, at least act like you do. Shake people's hands, ask them questions, and take business cards. Eventually you might actually get some confidence with all that faking!

Attitude in Action

Take a moment to think about your strengths and weaknesses. What qualities make you "you"? How can you utilize those qualities?

10

A Kick in the Attitude Principle #8

Courage Is the Defining Force That Conquers Fear, Average, and Bullies

Fear is a shadow, not substance.

—Judo Master Han

To say "live with courage" is easier said than done. It's a giant leap and one that often requires a push. I forget how old I was when it happened, but when my first tooth came loose, it was right on the edge of coming out. It wiggled back and forth to the point it was annoying. Mom and Dad suggested I pull it out right away. At that suggestion, I remember the tingle of fear running up the back of my spine in anticipation of pain and the unknown.

Fear is a beast that we often feed with worry and it grows into panic and anxiety.

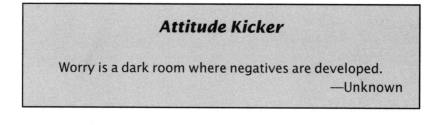

Attitude Kicker

Worry is a dark room where negatives are developed.

—Unknown

Fear has a way of introducing a person to himself. A majority of fear is made up of what we create in our imaginations. Fear can be a false representation of what really is.

After graduating from college, my brother and I rented a small apartment in an old building that came furnished with scary and odd sounds late at night. I remember getting up in the middle of the night to get a drink of water and seeing a shadow race through the hallway. My gut dropped to the floor and you could hear my heart beating in my chest like a drum. I stopped in my tracks and thought, "There is someone in the house! Now, wake up the entire building with your man-scream that sounds like a monkey who just had his banana stolen."

I made some sounds, then discovered that the light from the other room made my own shadow run down the hallway. It wasn't another human in the apartment; it was me. Yep, I was afraid of my own shadow. I let the weird sounds of the building play tricks on my thinking. That thinking turned to fear and it grew into worry, panic, and anxiety. Instead of living like a normal person, I was on the lookout for whatever I created in my imagination, even though there was nothing there. I created a false perception that got the best of me. That's what fear does, if you let it.

I think all of us can look back on certain scary moments growing up or throughout our adult lives that struck that chord of fear. The first time I got up to give a speech in high school, I was scared. Asking a girl out to prom, I was scared. Looking for work, I was scared. Starting over when my business failed, I was scared.

The point is, it's okay to get scared, but don't be controlled by the fear. Face what scares you and manipulates you into living with less than greatness. Here are a few strategies for using your attitude of courage to dissolve your fears.

Use Your Courage to Face Your Bullies

Dr. Maya Angelou, who overcame abuse to become one of the most legendary poets of all time, said to *Attitude Digest* magazine, "Look what you've overcome already. And some of the things no one ever knows but you. Some of the harassment and some of the bullying and some of the neglect that you've come through already, and still you say 'good morning,' and try to keep your body clean and wear clean clothes and speak in a decent voice . . . Look at what you've come through." The wisdom and courage you will gain in facing your fears will be invaluable to future encounters with adversity.

In the sixth grade, I encountered my first bully. He pushed other kids around and punched a lot of them to get lunch money. Nobody tattled on him or stood up to him because of *fear*. I avoided him at all costs. If he was walking down one hallway, I walked the longer way to get to where I needed to go.

At some point in life, you have to get tired of running from life's bullies. Donald Trump effectively says, "Don't take crap from anyone." As rough as that sounds, he tells you point blank: Don't be bullied by others. It's not good for you and not worth the esteem damage.

You are going to encounter a lot of bullies and have to summon courage to face them with reason, strategy, and good thinking. Bullies will make fun of you, put you down, do things that are not in your best interest, make up stories about you, or mock your way of life. They show up in the form of coworker, boss, stranger, relative, spouse, or neighbor.

You might get scared or think reactively. Both fear and reacting will not work in your favor. So what will?

Eventually, I did face the bully. But not without a dose of confidence, and strategy. I got some advice from a few people. Someone said, "Just fight him."

And I thought, "This guy could sit on me and they wouldn't find me for weeks."

My strategy was that if he wanted to fight me, I would challenge him to fight me in front of the principal of the school.

Here is how it played out. He wanted to fight me. I told him, "Good! If you want to fight me, let's see how tough you really are, and let's fight in front of the principal."

That seemed to freak him out. He never bothered me or my friends again.

You might say, "Well that's a good story, Sam, but how about me? How does that help me?" I've just shared a principle for facing your bullies. If you are being antagonized by a bully, you need to have confidence that you can prevail, overcome your fear, and think out a strategy for addressing the situation. Then, take rational action, using the best of what you know and have.

Years ago, I was watching a story on the news about two neighbors who went back and forth. One would dump something over the fence and the other would come out with a gun. It escalated to the point that someone got hurt, and it made the news! I encourage you to define a strategy that will address your bullies, rather than simply make them more angry. The difference is that when fighting fire with fire, there is still a fire. But with a strategy in play, you have the force of the fire department to put out the fire. That is living with courage.

Use Courage to Conquer Your "Average"

So, what is it for you? Is it potato chips late at night? Talking more than you listen? Procrastinating? Getting back at people? Being consistently late, easily annoyed, or non-empathetic?

What is your "average" that gets in your own way? I am not talking about a weakness you are born with. What I am addressing is your self-induced "average" that trips you up. Come on, you know what it is. Do you walk right, but talk left? Do you watch too much television? Courage to address your "average" is admitting you have something to work on, then going one step further to conquer it so it doesn't control you or have a negative impact on your life.

Do your best to define your average here.

The average I most need to conquer is: _____

_____

My action steps toward conquering my average:

1. _____

2. _____

3. _____

Use Courage to Overcome, Try Again, and Make a Comeback

Have you ever been thrown off a horse? I have! And my first thought wasn't, "That was interesting, I should get back up on the horse and do that again." The instructor insisted the horse could smell my fear and that I needed to exude confidence and get back up and on. No joke, I freaked out and ran to hide in a cornfield. But, because I reeked of fear, the instructor and the horse found me.

Life might throw you, like that horse did me. There are moments when we try something that didn't work, and develop a heart-stopping fear of trying again.

But for every one of those moments, there are chances to use courage to prevail. Can you think of someone who got thrown in life, but found a way to overcome the past experience, try again, and create a comeback?

We all love a good comeback story. Speaking of horses, let's talk about one of the most famous horses and the subject of one of the most inspirational stories of our time: Seabiscuit, a horse who symbolized hope for many during The Great Depression. A knobby-kneed horse who initially was seen as lazy, he struggled in races. Eventually, though, he found a trainer who understood him, and he slowly improved, and then excelled. Eventually, he won the coveted Triple Crown. In a subsequent race, however, he endured a ligament injury that outsiders thought would end his career. Amazingly, he healed, and yet again made a comeback, winning the Santa Anita Handicap. Seabiscuit had definite setbacks, but overcame the odds to win—more than once.

Use Courage to Ask For and Get What You Want

Have you ever wanted something, but been afraid to ask for it? There is a great book by Mark Victor Hanson and Jack

Canfield titled *The Aladdin Factor.* This is one of the best books I have ever read about asking for and getting what you want.

Even the Bible clearly says, "You have not, because you ask not," and, "Ask and you will receive."

Ask yourself this question: If you don't ask for the business, what will happen?

If you don't ask that special person out, what will happen?

If you don't ask for extra ketchup at the drive-through, what will happen?

. . . You miss out, is what happens.

We are afraid of rejection and everything that comes with it.

I know, rejection doesn't feel good, but let's say you knew for sure it would take 1,000 rejections to get to one yes, and that one yes would lead to you becoming a millionaire; would you do it? I'd bet you would at least consider it.

When I was 14, I needed what every kid needs at that age—extra money. We had a neighbor across the street who rarely mowed his yard. I saw an opportunity to make some extra money, and all I needed to do was ask if he wanted someone to mow his yard. The fear of rejection rattled around in my mind for hours. I stared over at this guy's house as the clock ticked. I even tried walking over to ask, but halfway over, I got scared and ran back home. Then I asked myself the right question, "If I *don't* go ask him about mowing his yard, what will happen? I won't make any extra money and I will miss out." With a racing heart, I walked over, knocked on the door, rang the doorbell, and knocked again. He wasn't home. I waited three hours until he arrived home, popped out from behind his bushes, and assured him I was a normal neighbor boy who was wondering if he wanted to have someone mow his yard for the summer.

To my amazement, he said, "I actually do!" Then he asked, "How much?"

Ahh man, I didn't think of that. What if I asked for too much? Fear set in again and I began to panic. Then I suggested $8 and he agreed. I found out later he would have paid me $20.

The good news is, once you face your fears—whatever they might be—you have a reference of overcoming and conquering something and are now equipped with the ability to do it again.

A few days later, I felt confident to ask other people if they needed their yards mowed. A few rejected me, but a lot of people said yes. The result was, I asked and got what I wanted. It takes courage to ask, but it reaps rewards.

My success has been built on this point. I ask people to help me, I ask for the business, I ask to get involved, I ask, ask, ask. Now, I don't always get a positive answer. But that's okay. I get more than enough yeses to wipe away the fear of worrying about rejection.

They key is, you have to prove it to yourself. Get out there and start asking for what you want, but ask with intelligence and ask those who are able to help you.

Attitude in Action

What area of your life—right now—requires some courage put to action?

I need to apply courage to this area of my life: _____

_____

Is there someone you know who can help push you to follow through or walk with you to help you find extra courage?

I am going to ask this person to help me:_____

_____

My plan to implement courage is:_____

_____

11

A Kick In the Attitude Principle #9

You Can't Move if Your Battery Is Dead—How to Give Your Attitude Muscles

The greatest secret is that we become what we think about all day long.

—Earl Nightingale

One day 10 years ago, I went for a jog to burn calories and stress. It was relatively warm when I set out for the quick run. I had been putting it off all day due to my very long to-do list. I had phone calls to make and projects to finish, and was feeling the stress. It was hitting me in every direction. I could feel my mood shifting to a negative one. I had such a pounding headache. I knew that I had been on this same schedule for weeks and my body was about to crash.

As I started jogging, I was reviewing the daily tasks in my mind and I became even more stressed. *Crack!* My ankle twisted. I fell to the ground and laid there in pain. I was no longer thinking about my to-do list, the phone calls, or what was stressing me out. The only thing that mattered was the searing pain in my ankle.

I was about a mile from home and knew that I could not walk that far. A farmer driving by saw me lying there at the side of the road and offered me a ride home. When I got home, I plopped right down on the couch with a bag of ice. The situation forced me to relax.

Later I went to the doctor to get my ankle checked. He told me I had a sprain and needed to ice it, stay off it, and relax.

There was a word I was not used to hearing: *relax*. How do you do that? My mind and body were not trained for such a thing. I was a magnet for stress and experiencing the effects of it physically and emotionally. My injury forced me to sit on the couch and do nothing. Well, not nothing—it forced me to relax. Once I gave in, my ankle got better, my energy level increased, my mood improved, and my spirit lifted—all thanks to a little relaxation.

One of the hardest life lessons to grasp is the need to take adequate time to slow down to renew ourselves and let go in order to get back to a place of strength. It's hard to live your best if you are running on fumes. We need time to rest, relax, think, reflect, and let go. If we don't take the time to release, our stress will begin to manifest itself in negative ways physically and emotionally.

The key to healthy living is not in waiting to be forced to rest, but in planning it with purpose. This is not easy. We live in times when we practice stress, rather than renewal, on a daily basis. We have to be aware of how harmful too much un-managed stress is and why renewing ourselves can be crucial in creating reserves to carry us through.

If I asked you to stand on one leg for a few minutes, I bet you could do it. But what if I asked you to stand on one leg for a few hours? Eventually, you would fall over from exhaustion. At first, the stress of standing on one leg would be manageable, but the longer you stood there, the more unbearable the strain would become, causing you to crumble.

We can only do so much of what we do without running into burnout. The stress can build to a place where we are no longer any good for ourselves, relationships, or work.

It's important to recognize the signs of needing renewal. Here are just a few: constant fatigue, moodiness, rage, frustration, depression, tense neck muscles, forgetfulness, headaches, and a spike in weight gain or loss. While these can also be symptoms of other underlying issues, taken as a whole they can also spell out an overly stressed person whose mind and body need some rest. Many of these factors can put us at a higher risk of heart disease. Plus, if we are running on fumes, our minds become magnets for negative thinking. We might carry around unnecessary thoughts that get blown out of proportion or be more prone to saying or doing something regretful. A lack of energy can feed your tiger (which I talk about later).

The lesson of needing to recharge ourselves is something we can see all around us. Think of your cell phone. I have to recharge mine every night when I get ready for bed.

What about when your kids get cranky? Our first thought is, *this kid needs a nap.*

Taking a necessary rest is a lesson we must grasp and apply to our lifestyle, no matter what we do.

What Are the Benefits of Recharging Yourself?

As I have mentioned in this book over and over, life gets better when we get better; this involves recharging our attitude batteries. We make life better when we operate from our best place, one of strength and energy. In order to do that, we have to recharge ourselves. The benefits are many. We become more productive, treat others with more respect, and take care of ourselves more effectively. The experiences we create for others and ourselves are of a higher quality. Our relationships improve. Our passion and enthusiasm are rekindled. We no longer carry around unmanaged stress that causes us to drag, but are energized and ready to get the best out of ourselves and life.

It is easier to maintain a good attitude than it is to try to fix or overhaul a bad one. The attitude you have boils down to a matter of choice. If you choose to maintain the right attitude, you are choosing to take the necessary steps to ensure your attitude stays right.

To best nurture our attitude, it is important to identify what can affect it in a negative way, so we can be prepared to defend ourselves from these stressors.

The four main attitude vultures that can make a good attitude vulnerable to becoming negative are:

1. Stress
2. Fatigue
3. Hunger
4. Negative influences—family, friends, reading or listening materials, and so on.

I am sure you have experienced each of these four at some time. Every day, we might encounter one of the four elements, or maybe all at the same time. And you may be the most positive person on the planet, but if your mind and body are encountering any of these elements, your attitude can be pulled to the dark side. Your dark-side outlook says, "Stay out of my way or endure my wrath!"

The value of knowing what these four elements are is that doing so equips you with the awareness to identify them when they first confront you, so you can do something about them before they make you negative. I think if we know what makes our attitudes turn south, we are better able to combat and nip those things in the bud before they get the best of us.

Corporations are beginning to understand how crucial our energy and health are to our production. Quest Diagnostics's employee wellness program has been honored as a leader for making health and wellness an integral part of the workplace. There are a number of interesting employee stories, (including that of Bill Germanakos, the 2007 season winner of the NBC television program *The Biggest Loser*), who attribute much of their daily success to Quest's focus on promoting healthy lifestyle changes.

Keep Your Attitude Batteries Charged Daily

I have found that following these easy steps allows me to keep stress out of my life—or at least manage it when it must rear its ugly head. They will work for you, too.

Go for a Walk

As you walk, let go of your day. Be in the moment. Take a few deep breaths. Do this on your lunch break if you can, or after dinner. When you work out on a consistent basis, your body releases endorphins, which relieve stress and actually improve the quality of your mood. Try to move for up to a good hour each day. Instead of taking the elevator, take the stairs. Try not to park so close to where you are going, but park far away and walk. Get a gym membership and use it. Get a workout partner, or hire a trainer to assist you in reaching your fitness goals. A body that moves creates positive energy toward your attitude.

Get Enough Sleep

Take a bath, play some soft music, read a magazine or book, anything that will move you into a tranquil state of rest. Also, naps are not just for kids. Thomas Edison, the great inventor, had a cot in his office. He would take 20-minute naps to recharge his mental energy. "Well," you may argue, "my employer won't allow me to bring a cot to work." I understand. The point is, fit in the recharge of a quick nap when you can. Perhaps if you get an hour for lunch and feel the need to close your eyes, set the alarm on your phone and take a few minutes to sit in your car or in the park—whatever it takes to get to your positive mental being. More rest equals more energy.

Plan Your Meals

When I get up, I plan all my meals for the day. When I do that, my eating habits become more manageable. Instead of over-eating or eating bad carbs when I need a pick-me-up, I plan small meals that energize the body (salads, celery, grilled chicken, tuna in a pouch, almonds, and lots of water). Eating the wrong foods, overeating, and not drinking enough water will block energy. Also, if you eat after 8:00 in the evening, your body will work all night to digest that food, so you will wake up tired. If you get the late night munchies (like I do), have some fresh fruit and yogurt in the refrigerator, ready for snacking.

Attitude Kicker

Take lots of fiber, fish oil, and omega 3s. Recent research has proven this can contribute to helping you feel more energized.

Get Out of Town

Plan a getaway. Do this often, not just once a year—if you can, perhaps once every few months. It doesn't have to be long. Just a day or two will do wonders. I personally enjoy getting away and fishing. I am always revitalized by sitting on the beach and watching the sunset and crashing waves.

Getting out of town (or even experiencing a different part of your own town) can help separate you from your world. That detachment is key to recharging yourself. There will always be things to get done—projects, deadlines, and the unexpected—but in order to face them with strength, you have to be at your best. Sometimes finding your best requires losing your worries in a fresh environment for a short time.

Do Nothing

Sometimes I do nothing and I get a lot out of it. I may just watch a good movie, sit on my porch, take a two-hour nap, play with my dog, or putter around the house on a project that will eventually involve me hiring someone to fix what I messed up. That's not being lazy; it's just me allowing myself to decompress in a restful and stress-free way. There are times when if you called me and asked, "What are you doing?" I would tell you, "Nothing, and loving it." Really, I am just resting, and not thinking about work, bills, or projects.

Pamper Yourself

Pamper yourself with something delightful. Doing this can rid your muscles as well as your mind of toxins that have built up due to stress.

Pamper yourself with:

- Calling and talking with a good friend
- A one-hour massage
- A good movie
- Taking a few deep breaths
- Exercise
- Eating something good
- A good book
- A warm shower or bath
- Some good tunes
- Painting
- Fishing.

What do you like to do to pamper yourself?

Identify the top three things you know that will relieve stress and relax you:

1. _____
2. _____
3. _____

Turn off Technology

Technology is taking over and becoming an obsession. I recently watched a program about a family that was challenged to remove technology from their house for two weeks. The mom was always on the computer. Dad was always on the couch watching television. The kids were always texting, often with each other and their parents in the same house. Some of us respond to every ring tone on our phone with an immediate, "*I gotta get that!*"

The results of this family taking a break from technology were very beneficial for them. The first week, however, was the hardest. They didn't know what to do with themselves. They got bored and stir crazy. But by week two, they began to take walks as a family, visit new places, eat dinner together, and yes, talk to each other!

Have you read the book, *The 4-Hour Work Week* yet? I encourage you to do so. It's about structuring your life in such a way that technology doesn't rule you. As author Timothy Ferriss's marketing states, "Forget the old concept of retirement and the rest of the deferred-life plan—there is no need to wait and every reason not to." Ferriss has won numerous awards, and lots of buzz for his business and life efficiency tactics, yet he checks his e-mails only a few times a day. He spends his spare time traveling and really living life, instead of just Googling about it. Ferriss's book teaches you how to use technology more effectively. Here are some tips:

- *Turn off your phone during meals.* That's a good start.
- *Limit your television viewing to a set amount of time.* Hey, I enjoy movies and funny sitcoms. But, I don't sit there for five hours staring blankly at a screen. I might watch something for 30 minutes and that's it; I am done. Growing up, my parents didn't allow my two brothers and me to watch television during the week. We had to play sports or do something positive for the mind. But today, this is more challenging. We have so many stations to choose from, we can grow addicted.
- *And most importantly, if you have a television in your bedroom, get it out of there and fast.* That is my recommendation, based on experience. Instead put a CD player or iPOD docking station in your room and play soothing sounds that calm your mind. The problem with television in the bedroom is that if you watch it before you go to sleep, you don't actually achieve effective rest. Have you ever had the weirdest dreams after turning off the television and going to sleep? You will toss and turn and get up feeling like you really didn't sleep much. The first week without the television in that room is tough—an adjustment, but when you do this, you will discover your resting time is more effective and you will feel more energized.

What Technology Is Ruling You?

What can you do starting this week (a simple plan), to rule your technology instead of it ruling you?

1. _____
2. _____
3. _____

Sing, Even Sing Badly

I know this one sounds off the wall, but it works. Sing. Play some loud music and wail to it. Move to it. I like singing to The Temptations's "My Girl." Even if you sound bad, that's okay. Sing. It will improve the quality of your mood (and maybe your voice). Just try it.

Take Your Attitude Vitamins

Yeah, I know I already said this, but it's important! Study attitude for a minimum of five minutes a day or whatever amount of time equals the time it takes you to bathe.

Close to 18 years ago, I bumped into a man by the name of Zig Ziglar—one of the world's most profound Christian inspirational speakers, who makes a living helping people translate their attitude into effective ways to improve their lives. And when I say I bumped into him, I mean I literally almost laid him out flat! I didn't know who he was, but I had been given a free ticket to hear him speak. Before the event, I was trying to find a seat; and in my hurry and excitement, without looking where I was going, I walked around a corner and ran smack into Zig himself. I apologized with great sincerity, cowered a bit, and waited for him to chew me out. But he had a great attitude about the situation. He just looked up at me and said, "Looks like you are in a rush there, big fella."

I said, "Yes, sir. I have a free ticket to listen to a speaker by the name of Zig Ziglar. I heard he's pretty good."

He looked up, gave me a classic Zig Ziglar smile and said, "Well, that's super good!" When I finally got to my seat, I was surprised to see that the very guy I had just about knocked over was now giving the speech. I actually have had the chance to talk with Zig since then on three different occasions. One conversation was over the telephone while I was still in college. I wanted to interview him for our university paper, and he called me at 5:30 A.M. to talk about attitude (a true attitude wake-up call!). Here is the wisdom that I gained about developing a healthy, life-changing attitude from Mr. Ziglar. He said something like this (this is my paraphrase): If you do not like the output in your life (meaning your attitude), then you must change the input (what goes into your mind). What you feed the mind will govern your thinking, which will determine your attitude.

Mr. Ziglar also told me that he read for an average of three hours per day. He said something to the effect of, "Sam, I realize what I put into my mind will come out through my words, actions, and attitude." By choosing to fill his mind with positive material, he was able to create his good fortune in life. This concept has stuck with me ever since; it reminds me how important it is to feed my life with the type of material and knowledge that I want to convey.

So I ask you: What is flowing through you and creating your attitude? Think about what you are allowing to influence your attitude. What is feeding your words, actions, thinking, and beliefs? Input creates output; so take a brief moment and think about your environment and what you are allowing to influence you.

Attitude Kicker

Your responses and reactions are an example of your influences. If you don't like your responses and reactions to circumstances, start by changing what impacts you—people, places, and what you read, listen to, and spend time doing. It can feel unnatural at first, but when you change something small like this, you begin to see big changes in everything around you.

Dig into the fundamental basics for your attitude. Read these books. They will reset, kick, jump-start, and rekindle your attitude. They are my personal favorites and I have read them all more than once. They are old school, and the information works when you put it into action.

Speak and Grow Rich, by Napoleon Hill

Rich Dad Poor Dad, by Robert Kyosaki

How to Win Friends and Influence People, by Dale Carnegie

Success University, by Og Mandino

Better Than Good, by Zig Ziglar

Attitude Is Everything, by Keith Harrell

Shut Up, Stop Whining, and Get a Life, by Larry Winget

Anything by Harvey Mackay, Les Brown, and John Maxwell

Anything by Anne Bruce (Her stuff kicks!)

Do a Mental Detox

Negative stuff gets in; that's a fact. You have to wash it out. Renewing your mind involves clearing out the garbage. It's like taking a shower every day. Your body gets that attention; now summon the discipline to do the same for your mind.

Experts tell us we should be drinking eight glasses of water a day. Why? Because it's fun to go the bathroom all day? No. It flushes our system of toxins. You are drinking that water to make your body healthy, to get rid of the junk that gets in there.

The same concept is true of our minds. We have to detoxify them or flush them daily. We do that by guarding what goes into our mind. By wisely selecting who we hang around with, what we choose to believe, and what we listen to, watch and read, we are selectively deciding to fill ourselves with only the best. Again, the more goodness you put into your mind, the more it will wash out the negative.

Detox Action: Listen to something positive.

These are some people whose audios I like to listen to over and over:

Zig Ziglar

Jim Rohn

Earl Nightengale

John Maxwell

Brian Regan (My all-time favorite comedian to lighten you up. He is clean and just hilarious.)

Sam Glenn (Sometimes I like to hear what I have to say!)

Use Uplifting, Empowering Words When You Talk to Yourself

Experts estimate that we talk to ourselves all day long, and 80 percent of our self-talk is normally negative. We beat ourselves up mentally, criticize ourselves, doubt ourselves, compare ourselves, and just lack the perspective of value in who we are based on what others have said or experiences we've had that were less than ideal. Change your self-talk. If you can, catch your inner dialogue in midstream and see what kinds of words you are using. If the tone is: "Why try?" "I could never!" "What's the use?" "I wish I could change this about my body," and so on, then you need to change your inner language. Write down some positive statements that involve words like "I can" or "I am" on a note card, and speak victory and empowerment into your life. Affirm your greatness and your potential.

Words are powerful, and you need to filter the words you hear around you as well. If you internalize the negative words people throw at you and play them over and over again until you start to believe them and own them, you block the door to your greatness. Instead, you have to release those words and replace them with truthful and empowering ones.

Also, it's okay to speak empowering words in advance. If today is a hard day, just say, "My day is hard now, but it's going to be awesome later."

You can quote scripture from the number-one selling book on the planet: the Bible. One of my favorite verses is Phil. 4:13: "I can do all things through Christ who gives me strength."

Of course, we all find our inspiration coming from many different sources. The important thing is to identify something that works for you.

Your self-talk is very powerful and important to get you feeling your best, doing your best, and going for your best. If you catch yourself beating yourself up with negative words, just take a moment to remind yourself of what you are doing, and get back to bettering your outlook with words that shine a light onto your path. If people ask, "Why are you talking to yourself?" just tell them what I tell them: "I like to talk to smart, good-looking people!"

Look for the Lighter Side in Situations

I know I'm repeating myself, but it's important. Notice I did not say, "Look for the light at the end of the tunnel." That would imply that you are in the dark now. Instead, see the light around you, where you are. Make the most of your current situation. Yes, some situations can be really stressful and perhaps tempt us to want to be negative—but in every situation there is a bright side waiting to be discovered. Take the time to look at the scenario from all perspectives and think about it.

It is also very important to ask someone or several trusted people to help you see what you are not seeing. Others can provide glimpses into a huge source of brightness. There are times when I have struggled with seeing the lighter side, and when I get the input of someone else, it opens my eyes to be more understanding and deal with things in a more effective and healthy way.

Limit Your Time with Toxic Attitudes (People)

Some people have poor and negative attitudes and don't even realize it.

Attitude Kicker

Misery loves company and it's always recruiting.

Remember, attitude is contagious. A toxic attitude can bring down a company in a day! A positive attitude can also spread like wildfire. Which one will you choose to befriend?

Be on guard for the attitudes that defeat you. These negative attitudes will keep you from your best. They are what turn a healthy attitude into a toxic attitude.

Collect Resources to Serve as Your Attitude Jumper Cables

These might be your favorite motivational quotes (your vitamins!), a close friend, or someone or something you know you can utilize during the storms of life to recharge yourself. Make recharging your emotional and physical batteries a priority. To be at your best, you have to be active about it. We are going to encounter stress on a daily basis, and too much of it left unmanaged can hurt us. If you try to get up the mountain on fumes, you are not going to make it. You won't be happy, and life will seem like a drag. Make the choice to slow down, let go, and get renewed. When you do, you will always come face to face with your best self.

Attitude in Action

In what areas can you take better care of your health, to nurture your attitude? What influences can you change, add, or subtract to create better input?

12

A Kick in the Attitude Principle #10

It's Not the Season, but How We Respond in the Season That Counts

It's not the load that breaks you down, it's the way you carry it.

—Lena Horne

Sometimes even when we have made the choice to change the picture of our lives, we get walloped in the head by some unexpected change or challenge. I know, because I've lived through a tornado. When I was in high school, the town where I lived was wiped off the map by a rare twister. My home was destroyed, but we all survived.

Even the strongest attitudes can be tested by storms. Adversity is an unscheduled appointment to wrestle with our attitude. The key is to not let the storm take control of our lives, but instead to use our attitude to navigate.

I don't want to mislead you about my approach to adversity. Let's be real; when it happens, it hurts. When you stub your toe, it's painful. But it's not the wall's fault. It happened; deal with it and move forward.

I don't know about you; but I'm fed up! I am mostly tired of listening to all the complaining around me. Turn on the television news or the radio, pick up a newspaper, and what do you see? Bad news. You look around and realize that people are very scared right now. They don't know what to expect. The housing market is awful; jobs are being cut; companies need bailouts; and the list goes on. One person told me his company laid off thousands of people; those who stayed had to take a 10 percent pay cut. Why? Some think it was so the company's shareholders could get paid, and the bottom line would look right. I don't care how you spin it; it's disturbing. We are at sea right now, and the weather isn't pretty. The wind carries bad news with it every day.

Despite this brutal information, I believe there is still one thing within us all that can defy the storm and bring us out ahead; and that is our attitude. I am not claiming that attitude is the end-all, be-all to solving world problems; but it is the greatest tool we have to control the direction of our individual lives, making things better and dealing with all the junk going on. I used to be a certified complainer, and then one day it finally hit me—it doesn't work. It doesn't direct your sail toward safety; a positive attitude does. When your sail is adjusted, you begin to travel in a new direction. The first thing to do is take action. If you are complaining about the wind, start directing that sailboat the way you want to go. Use your adversity to your advantage.

Attitude Kicker

When the market stinks, remember you don't have to.
When your real estate and stocks lose value, remember you
    don't have to.

> Your coworkers may be jerks, but you don't have to be one, too.
> And if you don't believe any of this—then so be it for you.

I would like to offer a few ideas that will help adjust your sail even in the roughest storms, and take you in a positive direction. Let's discuss a few methods that will help you use your attitude to get ahead when the wind is beating you back.

We cannot change the past (even if it was yesterday). We cannot change others, inflation, gravity, or the weather. The one change we can always make is to our attitudes; and that's a change that ultimately determines the kind of world in which we live, the direction in which we move, and the results that we attract. When you can alter your focus during a storm, you will be able to improve your direction in life. Creating the right mental outlook is vital to adjusting your sail.

Mind you, it's not about ignoring what's obvious, or repeatedly chanting, "There are no weeds in my garden." It's about choosing to look at circumstances differently, taking positive action, and moving forward in an upbeat direction.

If you are at a crossroads, this can be difficult. But you still have a choice, and it's simple. Realistically, you always have two directions to choose from, positive or negative. This may seem simplistic or very much like a generality, but think about it. It's true.

Attitude Kicker

Tony Hawk, pro skateboarder, believes in the power of a positive attitude. His attitude philosophy is to ride through the good and bad times and to embrace the challenge when there are bumps in the road.

Shift Is Going to Happen, so Deal with It

My flight from Chicago to Atlanta had been running behind, so we landed later than I had anticipated. I was in a rush to change and get ready to speak at an event. I wouldn't have time to change my clothes later, so as soon as I got off the plane, I went to the largest stall in the bathroom and began to do what Superman does in telephone booths—prepare for action. I unfolded my light brown suit; luckily there weren't too many wrinkles. I was almost ready—I only needed to tie my shoes and would be on my way.

At 6'7", it's just habit for me to set my foot up on something in order to tie my shoe. In this case, the only available surface was the toilet lid. While I worked on the left shoe, the toilet seat kept shifting back and forth. The back bolts were not tight, which caused a rather precarious situation. I carefully balanced myself and began to tie my right shoe. However, when I leaned my weight forward, my foot slipped right into the bowl. Water was everywhere—mostly on my suit. To say the least, I wasn't pleased.

Just as I was assessing the water damage to my pants, I heard a guy outside the stall yell something loudly for the entire restroom to hear. (Mind you that merely seconds before, the "Aaah—kerplunk! " and, "Oooh, *man!* It's everywhere!" was all that was heard by anyone outside my stall, without any visual context.) I didn't realize how vocal I had been from the perspective of anyone else in that bathroom, until I heard that guy blurt out, "Wow! That dude sure had to go!"

Everyone started laughing out loud—including me. I walked out and the same guy saw my wet pant leg and asked, "What happened to you?"

Jokingly, I responded, "I went for a swim! You know, I just jumped right in."

He laughed; I began to explain the faulty toilet with its improperly bolted seat, and how I attempted unsuccessfully to tie my shoe as that errant top kept shifting back and forth. This man then uttered the words I am fairly certain I will likely not soon forget. He looked at me as he was walking out, and with a big smile said, "Well, remember this, young man—shift happens!"

I still find myself laughing about that comment whenever I remember it; hence my purpose for writing something on this phrase (which has incidentally been trademarked by motivational speaker James Feldman).

One thing is for certain: Life is constantly shifting. Change is a given. You may agree with me when I say change can be uncomfortable, frustrating, and inconvenient; however, it has the potential to be a much more positive experience.

Some of us who are experiencing such a shift need a nightlight to guide our way. Do you remember how, as a little kid, going to bed could be one of the most terrible parts of the day? It meant that the lights would go out and we'd get a visit from that mysterious thing that was making noise under the bed or in the closet. Sure, Mom and Dad told us, "Don't worry; there's nothing under your bed or in your closet. Now go to sleep!"

It's at this point that every child in the world realizes that their parents are nuts! Only kids can see what lurks under the bed and in the closet, because they have vivid imaginations, which many people lose as they get older. My mom once told me that we went to church every Sunday; but I didn't remember that. However, I do remember going to a huge building every Sunday where I became Spider-Man for an hour, using my imagination to keep me entertained!

What saves almost every child from a frightful night is the glimpse of light from a cracked door, or my personal favorite: the Walt Disney nightlight. Light brings perspective; it brings a sense of safety. I still have a nightlight to this day. Now it's more to protect me from the wall that likes to jump out and have a toe-on collision with my foot; but the point is that if we can keep even a little light in our attitude, it will provide some illumination during dark times.

Here are a few ideas that I believe will assist you in your desire to maintain the right attitude during life's unexpected "shifts."

Stop feeling sorry for yourself and leave the pity party early.

I believe that you will agree with the fact that we often can't change certain circumstances. They are what they are. We simply cannot change certain people; they are too bull-headed. So what *can* you change? As always: Yourself.

When storms come, however, you don't have to let them take you wherever they please. You don't have to be on a blow-up raft tossing to and fro. You have some control. But you have to take action.

The first step is to not feel sorry for yourself and in turn become the victim. That won't get you anywhere but stuck. Make the decision to move . . .

Reinterpret Negative Information

As I've mentioned earlier, life will only give you information. If your dog dies, your house gets painted salmon pink instead of red, or your favorite underwear falls out of your suitcase in transit and gets taped to the outside, it all really only boils down to information. How you interpret that information will determine your outcome and results.

If you don't like your current situation, you need to begin by changing how you interpret information. That's how you begin to navigate out of this storm and achieve what you want in life. Some things that you desire are closer than you think. Sometimes despite adversity, all you need to do is tweak your attitude and you will be where you want, have what you want, and feel the way you want to feel.

You can choose to either set sail for misery and failure, or a better island. What you choose will have a dramatic impact on where you end up and what results you get.

Attitude Can Affect the Quality of All Seasons You Go Through

Does a positive attitude take away the junk that happens to you? No! Having the right attitude will assist you in keeping a positive perspective in adverse situations.

Michael J. Fox believes in the power of positive thinking when dealing with life challenges. He feels that while we may not have a choice about some things that happen to us, we have thousands of choices about how to respond to challenges. He has used this attitude to manage his Parkinson's disease and educate others.

Jonny Imerman, founder of the one-on-one cancer support organization Imerman Angels, believes that attitude is the wild card that can make the difference in getting through the biggest challenges in life. He advises others that life's challenges are not a sprint, but rather a marathon, and a strong attitude is what keeps the chin up at each mile marker along the way. Imerman states, " . . . I was diagnosed at 26 with testicular cancer, beat it at 27 after surgeries and chemo, relapsed at 28, then beat it again with an 11-inch surgery through my stomach! As life's challenges are not a sprint, but rather a marathon, STRONG ATTITUDE is what keeps the chin up each mile marker along the way . . . I needed my chemo, but I couldn't have done it without an ATTITUDE of NO DEFEAT. It's all about OVERCOMING challenges, one at a time!!"

Scott Hamilton, Olympic gold medalist and cancer survivor, believes in the importance of attitude, feeling that the only disability in life is a bad attitude.

Maybe You Don't Have It Quite so Bad

Someone once shared a very profound statement that changed my thinking and focus in the midst of a personal storm. I was in high school and my basketball coach said to me, "Sam, you need to stop feeling sorry for yourself. Someone somewhere has it a *lot* worse than you."

I hadn't thought of it that way; I had merely been focusing on myself and *my* problem. That single comment gave me a new point of view. Instead of feeling sorry for myself, I realized I should feel thankful. Of course, I didn't celebrate the fact that someone, somewhere had it worse than I did, but I can honestly tell you even now as I look around, I realize it is true. No person is an island; we all face challenges, and the reality is some seem worse than others. The purpose of acknowledging that someone somewhere has it worse than you do is to get your head out of your own situation so that you can begin to be thankful for what you *do* have.

Utilize Your Attitude Jumper Cables

During a storm you may need your Attitude Jumper Cables. I have a few physical reminders in place that I put in front of myself when I feel my thinking heading south, and they cause me to pause and stop the road trip to Mount Self Pity. One powerful tool is an article that I have posted on the magnet board in my office about a gentleman named Viktor Frankl. His 1946 book, *Man's Search for Meaning*, chronicles his experience as a concentration camp inmate and describes his methods of finding a reason to live. Frankl concludes that the meaning of life is found in every moment of living. Life never ceases to have meaning, even in suffering and death. He also points out that his reactions to his experience are not solely based on the conditions in which he lived, but rather on freedom of choice. Frankl also states that everything can be taken from a man except for the last of human freedoms— the freedom to choose one's attitude in any given set of circumstances, to choose one's own way. This is an incredibly powerful reminder for me, which quickly helps me recharge my kick.

Realize the Rescue Boat May Not Look Like What You Expect

A fella was sitting on his roof, because the flood waters had gone up so much he was forced to get to the highest part of the house. Some people came by in a boat and asked him if he wanted to get in and row to safety with them. His reply was, "No, God will save me."

A few hours went by, the water kept rising and a helicopter hovered over, sending down a ladder so he could climb up to safety. Again, the man declined, saying, "God will rescue me."

A few hours went by and the Coast Guard showed up and attempted to rescue the man. His response again was, "No worries; God will rescue me."

Finally, the water rose so high the fella drowned. When he came face to face with God in heaven, he asked God, "Why didn't you save me?"

God's response, "I tried. I sent you a boat and a helicopter, what else did you want?"

Be ready to take action to get out of your situation, regardless of the delivery method.

Attitude Kicker

Some of us just wait around for things to get better, instead of moving or acting in a way that could rescue us from our situation. Although it may seem like things are out of your control, the one thing you always control is your attitude. If you need to lose 10 pounds, the government isn't going to do it for you; *you* need to do it. Take action, get up, and move. Create a plan. Work it. Network. Run. Walk. Read. MOVE!

Take Action and Don't Let Excuses Sink Your Boat

If you want to sink your lifeboat, all it takes are excuses, which are essentially holes that are shot into it. So why do we make them? I can only assume laziness, or a desire to evade responsibility. If you pause for a moment and look around, you can learn about stories of people who don't have a great deal of talent, experience, or education; yet they are succeeding in life. For example, I met a woman who used to sell real estate. When things started going south, she found herself broke and very depressed. She wasn't sure what to do. However, she didn't make excuses; she instead conducted an inventory of what she could do and offer to others in order to make money. Since the job market wasn't great, she went into business offering herself as "A Wife for Hire." Yup, that's even what it says on the side of her car. She runs errands, helps plan parties, and will do just about anything her clients need to take stuff off their plates. She is busier and making a bigger profit than she was before, and enjoying the ride.

Another guy I know was recently let go after 26 years with the same company. The firm went under, and he was left with very little. He could have made excuses about why his situation was bad; but instead, his experience pushed him to act on his lifelong desire to work with animals. He started a doggy motel, and is now enjoying great success doing something profitable, about which he is extremely passionate.

You don't need to hit rock bottom, and you don't need a bail out; what you need is to get a clue. You have greatness in you just waiting to be put into action. What gifts do you have that if acted on would take you to new and exciting places? Is there one thing you can do today to improve your life?

Start by Asking These Questions

The right questions that will help you adjust your sail to go in a right direction.

- What will I lose if I don't change my attitude? Where will the current storm take me?
- Who or what do I need to stop blaming for the state of my attitude?
- What is one thing I can do today to begin to adjust my own sail?
- What do I need to do so I am not hung up and hung out to dry?

Six Bonus Ways to Profit from Change

1. *Realize right away that there is a gift in every failure.* Or, said a different way, there are opportunities in every adversity. The gift of failure is that sometimes our life purpose can come from the ashes of whatever it is that

we've lost. When something doesn't work out, we have to be willing to rebuild, get up, and try again. Getting thrown off the horse isn't fun; but sometimes it means that a better horse is out there waiting for us. Kristin Armstrong was a Junior Olympian in swimming when she was diagnosed with osteoarthritis. Instead of quitting life, she started bicycling as therapy, and went on to win a gold medal in cycling at the Olympics. She found the "better horse," through her adversity.

2. *Act with courage.* I've said this before, but it's important enough to repeat here. When life sends us an unscheduled appointment with hardship, it's easy to get scared and react with fear, discouragement, and doubt. I remember the day that I received a phone call from a creditor about a bill that I couldn't pay. I had no money. I was so scared I sold my truck the next day; and the result was I had no way to get home or to work. I was worse off, because my fear got the better of me. Acting with courage empowers us to gain the confidence to know that we can conquer our challenges.

3. *Be grateful.* It's easy to feel sorry for yourself when things are going badly. But the fastest way back to a perspective of clear thinking is through looking at what you *do* have. Take out a piece of paper and write down everything you can be thankful for right now. It might only be that you have a toothbrush, shoes, a pillow, a friend, or a blue sky outside. Put that paper in your pocket or post it somewhere where you can easily see it. Refer to it often, whenever you feel yourself beginning to throw a pity party for yourself. Use it as part of your Attitude Jumper

Cable Kit (check out EverythingAttitude.com for more ideas to throw into your kit).

4. *Remind yourself that this, too, shall pass.* Your present situation *is not permanent*; life keeps moving. If we think life will never get better, our thoughts become unhealthy. The words and actions that follow often create a defeated mentality that limits our potential and power to achieve. I believe there is a season to mourn, grieve, and acknowledge our pain or situation; but when the season is over, it's over. Move on. It's time for a new season of rebirth, with new choices, new thinking—the works.

Attitude Kicker

Here are some great tidbits of wisdom on adversity from a recent article, "A little adversity, a lot of success," by business motivational speaker Harvey Mackay (distributed by United Feature Syndicate, Inc., 2009).

Adversity is the grindstone of life. Intended to polish you up, adversity also has the ability to grind you down. The impact and ultimate result depends on what you do with the difficulties that come your way. Consider the phenomenal achievements of these people who experienced extreme cases of adversity.

- Beethoven composed his greatest works after becoming deaf.
- Thomas Edison had an IQ of less than 100, almost died of scarlet fever and was nearly deaf, yet he became one of the greatest inventors in history.

- If Columbus had turned back, no one could have blamed him, considering the constant adversity he endured. Of course, no one would have remembered him either.
- Abraham Lincoln became one of our greatest U.S. presidents, despite dropping out of grade school, going broke, having a son die at a young age and running for political office and losing four times.
- Carol Burnett, another Horatio Alger member, was raised by her grandmother because both her parents suffered from alcoholism. She lived in an impoverished area, was divorced twice, yet went on to great success and her variety show won 23 Emmy Awards.
- Glen Cunningham was seven years old when he was so badly burned in a schoolhouse fire that his doctor said, "I doubt if he'll be able to walk again." Yet he went on to become the outstanding miler of his time.
- Nature is full of wonderful examples of how adversity fosters strength.

  -Botanists say that trees need the powerful March winds to flex their trunks and main branches, so that the sap is drawn up to nourish the budding leaves.
  -Pearls form inside the shell of certain mollusks as a defense mechanism to a potentially threatening irritant such as a parasite inside its shell. The mollusk creates a pearl to seal off the irritation.
  -And it was Ralph Waldo Emerson who pointed out, "When it is dark enough, you can see the stars."

  I don't like adversity any more than the next guy, but I welcome it. It has made me stronger, more fearless, and ultimately, more successful. Stare down adversity and watch it blink.

   Mackay's Moral: A smooth sea never made a skillful sailor.

5. *Create a new perception for your life.* Affirmations of a new perception for you can be:

   I am no longer a victim, but a victor.

   I am more than able to overcome this situation.

   I am bigger than my failures!

   I was born with the ability to achieve and live my dreams.

   I have options and solutions.

   I am going to get up and make something happen today!

6. *Stop complaining about it!* When a "shift" occurs, our first inclination is often to fight, resist, and complain about it. But these aren't productive reactions. When external changes occur at work or in your personal life, your perception of how to deal with them can often become distorted by those initial urges. It's easy to complain; but there is no power in doing so. *Complaining has no real effect on the situation, aside from hurting your attitude and making you feel poorly.* Complaining does not plug the leak that can sink your boat. When things get bad or change in an unfavorable way, you must consider—before falling into the trap of complaint— *what are you going to DO about it?*

   Change can be threatening, but if used in the right way, can also be the tool for the greatest growth. Often the biggest obstacles become the instruments by which we gain the greatest skills.

Attitude in Action

What is one possible gift that may come from your current adversity?

13

A Kick in the Attitude Principle #11

Give Yourself Permission to Dream Big Dreams

We have the power to shrink our dreams to fit reality or the power to stretch our reality to fit our dreams.

—Anonymous

Let's say we are on a hunting trip. We come to the edge of the forest and instead of going into the forest to hunt snipe (I have never seen one, but I have been told they are out there. Some of you will get that. Yep, I fell for it.), let's say I was just to shoot random bullets into the forest with the hope of hitting something. Do you believe that would be highly effective in nailing my target?

No, of course not. Why do so many fire so aimlessly with their dreams? They wish upon the stars, yet don't actually have a plan for arriving.

You can shoot at the stars, but in order to be effective, you also need a plan for reaching them. Better yet, you need to identify your target star. Simply put, know what you want. It's called having a goal.

One guy years ago told me he hated to set goals, because if he didn't reach them, he was disappointed and miserable. While I can understand that, it is also not very effective. Wouldn't you rather aim for the moon and miss, than aim for a pile of mud and hit?

Tips for the Realization of Goals and Dreams

On average, I give close to 90 speeches per year. I didn't, however, set out to be a speaker. If fact, I actually took low grades in college, just so I wouldn't have to give a speech at graduation. A few years after I graduated from college, I volunteered with a youth program, and I was eventually asked to share a few encouraging words to the students. I did, and I stank!

I enjoyed inspiring others, however, and saw real value in what I was doing. I wrote down my goal of becoming an inspirational speaker, but it didn't happen overnight. Let me highlight something here. Taking the following steps after writing out my goals helped me go from sleeping on my mom's living room floor at nights, working as a nighttime clean up guy, to speaking to audiences as large as 75,000 people—all in less than a year and half. How does that happen? Here are the philosophies that put the reach in my attitude.

Philosophies drive our attitude. Some of us don't really know what's driving our attitude. You have to clearly define your philosophies. Here are mine.

Take the Stairs—the Elevator Is Out of Order

When it comes to achieving your dreams and goals in life, taking the stairs will help you learn and grow and pick up valuable insights along the way.

Mac Anderson, founder of the company Successories, didn't start out with a plan to print motivational quotes on pretty pictures for the world to purchase. Instead, he printed a small quote book for a group. It was so well received that he printed more. Eventually, he placed a small ad in the back of the books for those who wanted to order quotes on plaques. When that took off as well, he put the quotes on beautiful prints—and thus Successories was born, and continues to grow today. If he hadn't started small and "taken the stairs," going through the motions of testing small products as he went, learning from his achievements and errors, he never would have achieved his current level of success.

You Don't Have to Be Great to Start, but You Have to Start to Be Great!

The key to any goal or dream is to start somewhere. If someone is achieving success, they started. You have to take the first step. Will you have some fears? Sure, it's a part of the process. Will you fail and be criticized along the way? Yep! To achieve what you want, you have to travel through the land of fear, criticism, rejection, and failure to get to your destination. But, it's so worth it!

I would guess that most people give up because someone talked them out of their dreams, or they just couldn't handle the land of rejection, criticism, and failure.

Being a speaker, it's a given that not everyone is going to like my message, style, or look. I used to care about that. Now, I don't. And I believe that's why I continue to succeed. My program is solid. If someone doesn't like me, the issue isn't with me, it's with them. Maybe they aren't ready for my message or we aren't a good match. That is okay, though, because I know that I still help many people, and that keeps me going.

When you are going after a dream with passion, people will try to put you down. And sadly, it's often the people close to us like friends and family who can have the most effect on our confidence in this area.

A Barking Dog Doesn't Chase Parked Cars

People are going to say what they want about you, your goals, or your dream. So, let them. Tune them out. Some will rain on your parade because they don't have one. Larry Winget, author of *People Are Idiots and I Can Prove It*, clearly proves this concept in his book. Some people will be idiots and try to get in your way, block you, guilt you, pull you down, and step on your every positive effort and move. It is in your personal power and attitude to defy and silence the barking dogs of the present and the ones in the past that perhaps pop up from time to time.

Passion Fuels the Drive

I enjoy watching Donny Deutsch's program, *The Big Idea*. His guests each had an idea, and instead of sitting on it, acted on it. I get inspired by what the participants went through to achieve success. You can hear the passion in their voices. Passion for what you do or acting on a dream is a form of enthusiasm, excitement, and energy. It fuels the drive. You gotta have it! If your dream doesn't infuse you with passion, get a new dream.

Whether you like and agree with him or not, one thing you have to admit is that Glenn Beck has passion. Day after day, he captivates audiences on radio and television with his passion. And it permeates through the airwaves.

Have Goals and a Dream

Goals and dreams give birth to hope, purpose, and positive expectations. If you want a reason to get up and get moving, have a goal or a dream that you feel gives you purpose and includes a positive expectation for your life.

Stop Being a Nut—Get Out of Your Shell

What I mean by this is, expand yourself to move past your comfort zone. Most people never achieve what they want because it's too uncomfortable to try. Take small steps. Ask yourself, "What's the worst that could happen if I do it?"

"What is the best that could happen?"

"What will happen if I don't do it?"

"What will I miss out and lose out on if I don't do it?"

"What will I gain if I do it?"

Jeff Bezos, the founder of Amazon.com, had a great job in software on Wall Street when he got the idea to sell books online. He knew there was a 70 percent chance that he would fail, but something made him try anyway. "I knew that if I failed, I wouldn't regret that," he has said. "But I knew the one thing I might regret is not ever having tried. Most regrets are acts of omission and not commission." He had courage and conquered his fear, taking a big risk, which paid off. It takes courage to confront the enemy of average. Average keeps you in the zone; courage pushes you out of the zone.

Keep Moving

Change can knock you off your goal's path, but you can make the detour work for you—just keep moving.

I really enjoy the groups who book me to speak. I know when a group hires me, they value that attitude makes a difference and realize that what jumper cables are to a car battery, I am to an event.

What I enjoy even more about the events, however, is talking with people about their businesses and what successes and challenges they encounter. As the economy has changed, so have the strategies of many I have met. Several have lost jobs and gone entrepreneur.

Jim Collins, author of *Built to Last* and *Good to Great*, defines entrepreneurship as a life concept, an opportunity to show your strength, manage risks, and make money.

I work with a lot of direct sales groups. What inspires me most about them is seeing the courage and the passion in their members' eyes and attitudes. When I meet a sales associate from Mary Kay Cosmetics, for example, I meet a positive attitude in action.

Robert Kyosaki, author of *Rich Dad, Poor Dad*, says he made his fortune in real estate, but if he had to do it all over again it would be with a direct sales organization. You can earn a great income doing this while helping a lot of people.

There are some great organizations whose history and stories I really admire, like Mary Kay Cosmetics and Pre-Paid Legal. When I talk with people who sell directly, they understand that their success is based on their attitude and effort.

Most people who get involved in some form of business like this get all pumped up, but then fizzle out faster than a shooting star. Why? Their attitude and effort fall apart, and as a result they give up and move on to something else.

When change happens, it can be uncomfortable and even inconvenient, sure, but it doesn't have to be the end of the world as you know it. Change is a call to action, to be more innovative and creative in what you can do or offer. A goal will help you stay on task, to keep moving ahead.

Significance Means Nothing without Contribution

It's important that your goal involves a contribution of some sort as well, so that it will have universal meaning and "stick power." You will be more motivated to continue achieving if you know that you are helping others as you go.

Get Smart with Your Money

There are a few areas I see a lot of people struggle with and the big one is money. Get smart with your money. Don't ignore it or panic over it. You need to have a plan for paying bills, and spending and earning income. If you are starting a business, solicit help from an analyst to ensure that you have a solid plan for growth. Get advice from a financial advisor on how to invest, save, and profit. Your money needs a plan, because without one, it controls you.

Attitude Works Better with a Set of Skills

The right attitude is vital to anything worthwhile in life, but it's not the end-all be-all. What do I mean by that? I have a great attitude, but you don't want me to do your taxes, perform surgery on you, or fly the airplane. If there is a direction, vocation, or craft you want to move into, you have to acquire the skills to do so. And it's your attitude that will help you work through those skills. The combination of both working as a team will create the results you want.

Attitude in Action

This one will take years to complete but start today.

1. Identify your goals and dreams (short-term and long-term), and write them down. "Ink it if you think it," is what Mark Victor Hanson, coauthor of *Chicken Soup for the Soul*, says. What are they? Pour yourself a cup of joe, Diet Coke, or Fresca, get comfy and spend 20 to 30 minutes jotting down some plans and direction for your life: where you want to travel to, who you would like to meet, what fear you want to overcome, what new skill you want to learn, what organization you want to get involved with, what you want to be remembered for, and so on.

2. Be realistic about your goals and put a deadline on each of them.

3. Create an action plan with strategies. Start small, so that you have some easier successes to keep you motivated. Begin to construct a plan around your dreams and goals.

4. Take action on your plan.

5. Refine your (plan) strategies if something is not working, until you get to your destination.

6. Be persistent and don't give up.

14

A Kick in the Attitude Principle #12

The Strength of the Wolf Is in the Pack and the Strength of the Pack Is in the Wolf

No one succeeds alone.
> —Ray Kroc, founder of McDonald's

A friend of mine once invited me to dinner, and asked me how I would describe my perfect day. I didn't have to think long. "I would spend the entire day with all my friends and family, including the dysfunctional ones because every party needs entertainment—hence me."

Then it hit me. My perfect day boils down to one word, "relationships." Without meaningful relationships, your life suffers in emptiness. A positive relationship is one that gives us life and a heart of gratefulness.

Little Things Count Big

Identify the relationships that are most meaningful to you—family, friends, and colleagues.

If each relationship was a plant, what state would the plant be in? Think about what you do to contribute to the relationships that you value.

Little things that count big are:

1. *Spending quality time counts big.* It can be time listening, laughing, sharing, whatever grows life into the relationship. The biggest regret people have when they lose someone is, "I wish I had spent more time with him." We can't spend all the time doing what we want, so invest in the growth of the relationship by doing something the other person wants to do. Be in the moment and apply the time as a small thing that counts big. Remember, actions speak louder than words.

2. *Small acts of generosity count big.* A healthy focus of a positive relationship is not what you will get out of it when you put something into it, but what you can give. It's always good to get a reciprocation of some sort, but let your actions be a gift from you. Maybe this means buying someone lunch, washing someone's car, mowing someone's yard, folding the laundry, sending a cheesecake to someone's office—you get the idea.

3. *There are three words that count big.* Don't be afraid to say these three powerful yet often humbling words, "I am sorry." It takes a big person to know he is wrong, and an even bigger one to admit it and apologize. You have to humble yourself, which means putting down your pride and stubbornness to say you're sorry, so the relationship can continue to grow. If you have a disagreement about something, find a way to common ground, but expect to

give up some ground. If you don't, more things can go wrong, like in this story that was sent to me.

The Silent Treatment

A man and his wife were having some problems at home and were giving each other the silent treatment. The next week, the man realized that he would need his wife to wake him at 5:00 A.M. for an early morning business flight to Chicago. Not wanting to be the first to break the silence (*and lose*), he wrote on a piece of paper, "Please wake me at 5:00 A.M." The next morning the man woke up, only to discover it was 9:00 A.M., and that he had missed his flight. Furious, he was about to go and see why his wife hadn't awakened him when he noticed a piece of paper by the bed. The paper said, "It is 5:00 A.M. Wake up."

The strength of the wolf is in the pack and the strength of the pack is in the wolf. Having meaningful relationships is important because we can offer our strength to others and draw upon theirs when life hits us with a wrench.

Surround Yourself with a Circle of Encouragers

People will either increase us or decrease us. We need to surround ourselves with "increase" people—those who love us, encourage us, help us, and give us wisdom when we are struggling to think on our own.

There are some people who come into our lives and do things for which we can never repay them. I find the best way to honor those people is by giving thanks, living right, thinking right, doing right, and paying it forward.

My close friend Andy Warcaba, who I mentioned earlier had taken me for the cup of coffee that put a kick in my attitude, got me an autographed book titled, *Tough Times Don't Last, But Tough People Do*, by Dr. Robert Schuller. There was also $300 with it! What a gift. His encouragement was fuel to keep going when all my challenges were telling me to admit defeat. And even though I had no way to repay him for his generosity, I realized that's not what he wanted. His repayment would be me living my dream, giving my best, and doing the same in kind for others.

Another close friend, Steve Dawidiuk and I first met when I was a nighttime cleanup guy. The company I worked for rented the building from Steve. There was a lot of extra space, so I would set up my chalk art easel and practice drawing. Nobody could go in or out of the building without seeing all my artwork. Steve happened to notice my pictures and take interest in what I was doing. I told him about my passion to work with people who believe that attitude makes a difference. We developed a great encouraging relationship.

Even though almost a decade has passed, we still meet several times a year, not just for idle chitchat, but for some of that authentic and empowering talk—the kind that juices one's attitude. We meet at the Pancake House to eat flapjacks and talk life, business, struggles, and just about everything you can imagine. These moments are filled with huge amounts of encouragement and calories (one of which I am more thankful for than the other). For nearly 10 years, Steve and his family have graciously supported me with encouragement, prayers, and financial contributions to assist in projects that make a difference in the lives of others. I can only repay him by applying the positive example he has provided me and doing it for others. I also repay his efforts by giving my best efforts, including giving you my best.

What you need to know is this: My success in life is not a result of one man, me. I will never declare myself "self-made." I am successful because of people like my family and friends who unconditionally support me. Their contributions of love, encouragement, support, and integrity are what fuel me to go the distance, when everything else might say throw in the towel.

Take an inventory of those who increase you. Embrace and value your circle of support—even if it's only one person. Don't take it for granted—ever! If you feel like you don't have anyone in your life, go out and be a support to someone. Whatever you send out, it will come back. If you need love and encouragement, then give it first and it will return to you in ways that you cannot possibly imagine!

Some People Just Don't Fit into Our Lives

It's tough on the heart when a relationship doesn't work out in the way you have hoped. This is a sensitive subject and I will give you my take on it. There are some people who hurt us, often the ones closest to us. My take is not to complain about what you tolerate. I have had people treat me so poorly, it breaks the heart to comprehend. Instead of being bitter, I embrace the lesson and use it as a compass of wisdom.

Maybe you have had a relationship—personal or professional—and you did what I did: gave it my all—time, generosity, and love—and in return got my butt handed to me on something less than a silver platter.

You have to be careful, because there are some people who will play you like a game and tease your emotions and manipulate you to think or make choices that are not good for you. You are in charge of your personal happiness—you own that right—and if someone is messing it up in a violent, unethical, or abusive way, you have to put a stop to it.

I always suggest that before you act, think first. Get someone to help you think clearly about your situation. I recommend seeking professional advice on what actions you can take and how to get your mental stability back intact, when someone has clearly shaken it up with negative behavior.

I personally have had to limit time with certain people because they are negative, and the words they use and the actions they take do not align with my values. No, I am not being judgmental. Everyone has their own worth and reasons for their behavior. A few years back I had to learn the hard way to draw some boundaries for my life. Without them, people can run all over you. I had to clearly ask myself and define: What am I no longer willing to tolerate in relationships? I realized I didn't want to be around someone who put me down, or made me feel bad about myself or life.

You may have to have that heart to heart with someone to discuss why the relationship was in poor shape. Is it you? Is it them? Is there a way to repair it? You may have to air it out and address the elephant in the room.

There are people I still love dearly, and keep in touch with somewhat, but don't spend time with because it's not healthy or good for me. I don't allow them to engage me in a debate about it, either.

And sadly, there are some people to whom I have had to say goodbye. It didn't work out for some reason or another. I choose not to dwell on it and have it ruin the present and future. Instead, I acknowledge that it didn't work, and move on.

Make Peace with Your Past so It Won't Screw Up the Present

You can either get bitter or get better. I know it is a bit of a cliche, but it is a true statement. So, what's it going to be?

A part of me thought about listing everyone—the people, the companies—that have taken advantage, deceived, lied, obtained money that was not properly earned, or demonstrated unethical practices in working with me. I have a good-sized list, but bitterness isn't the cornerstone of living a positively charged life. You don't want to be going into new relationships with a bitter attitude. That's bad baggage, so make some peace with your past.

We can't control the practice of ethics—doing what is right—in others. I've had people say exactly what I wanted to hear, only to have their actions not match their words. The result of working with or developing relationships with people who lack integrity is that people get hurt. People lose money. Then it's hard to trust again.

But no matter the size of your pain, it is wasted energy to try and get even or show someone up. Revenge often ends up costing you more.

Practice Forgiveness

This may be the hardest action of all, but the value of this is for you. You need to find and make the peace, lest whatever happened eat you up on the inside for a long time. Sometimes people close to us will make little mistakes that let us down; we need to find the courage to forgive and not carry the weight of what happened. If it is possible to resolve the situation in a healthy way, then do that.

If something is beyond your control, I personally might suggest seeking legal counsel. This should be the last option and not one I favor. But if the situation is out of control, this is a healthy action. I am not suggesting that you become sue-happy; that's wrong. But justice will find a way of catching up to those who are unethical—for every action, there is a consequence and the snake eventually will bite those who do wrong. You may not see it, but it will happen.

If you have ever been let down and think, *"I can never trust again,"* I want to let you know that it is okay to trust again. Not everyone is out to get you, and you will find that not everyone will let you down. You just have to be careful. Each situation of letdown teaches you to become wiser. Carry the discernment with you to situations in your future.

What about When We Let Others Down?

It's a given. We are human and we are going to mess up. If you are making the same mistake over and over and over again, then something is wrong. But if you mess up, know it, want to fix it, and are sorry for your actions, then take action to fix what you can. Do what you can to right the wrong. If you broke someone's trust, don't expect it back for a very long time. That's a given. But you can seek his or her forgiveness. And he or she may or may not forgive you. Some things can't be fixed. Either way, you have to embrace the decision and the outcome, as you are the one who messed up. You need to own the result of your actions.

Success Means Nothing if You Are Standing Alone

Okay, don't take that point and twist it. I don't mean that if you work hard and move up the ladder of success you will be alone. Success is not fun if you're alone. It's more enjoyable if there are others with you. So bring others along with you, helping them, and letting them help you. Zig Ziglar says, "You can only get what you want if you help enough other people get what they want." I like this statement and know it to be true.

Years ago, I worked for a company whose owner, instead of knocking people down when sales were down or adversity showed up, would always ask employees, "What can I do to help you achieve something? Is there anything I can do better for you?"

And he would close almost every meeting by asking whoever was in the room, "Is there anything I can do for you?"

What did his actions build in that company? Loyalty. Commitment. Communication. Clarity. And my favorite, teamwork!

Networking Is about Building Positive Relationships

Positive relationships lead to win/win opportunities, so get out there and network and build some positive relationships.

Everyone has a story; get to know it. I used to be deathly afraid of networking events. I am an introvert my nature, which surprises a lot of people. But I get shy at all kinds of functions. What my life and business were lacking were better relationships. So I got out there, got a few CDs on how to strike up a conversation and how to work a room without being stupid drunk, stuff like that. Then I just went for it. I have met some amazing people who have helped me reach my goals and I have helped others reach theirs. Positive relationships are the key to great success.

I have been incredibly thankful for the networking efforts of a fellow motivational speaker and author, Anne Bruce, who not only has an incredible message about finding true north and taking the leap (check out her books!), but has also been a tremendous cheerleader. Instead of seeing me as a competitor, she has embraced my career and encouraged me, going so far as to market my speaking at her events, calling my staff even during her off time to ensure that she shares any wisdom she can to help my career. She has introduced me to numerous others who have helped me. She is one of the reasons I have brought this book to a publisher. I am incredibly grateful for her generosity, which has made me want to return the favor. We have published her articles in *Attitude Digest* magazine. I hope you all look her up today and book her to speak, or buy her books! Do you see how the attitude of giving to others can pay off, when it comes to networking?

Are you nervous when it comes to networking in person? Here is my little technique to help you work any room . . . Pretend you are a talk show host. Watch some talk shows and notice that the hosts are not sitting there talking about themselves. They are engaging the guests to talk about themselves.

When you walk into a room, just pretend it's part of the show and your job is to host people and make them feel comfortable, and open up. It works every time for me. I can walk up to total strangers and strike up a conversation. Basically, I get them to talk. And I have learned that people love to talk about one thing the most—themselves. And when you are finished talking with them, they like you more. Why? Because you talked about them. The psychology behind it is that they feel connected to you now. It's a gem and an excellent way to network and build new friendships.

Teamwork Is Vital to Achieving Any Form of Success

Close to eight years ago, I began to network with Jocelyn Godfrey, now editor-in-chief of *Attitude Digest* magazine. I began to seek her advice on how to grow my company, Everything Attitude. Over the years, I found such value in her consulting advice and the fact that she has always had my best interest at hand, that she now runs EverythingAttitude.com (my product and communications company). She is a team player. I cannot do what she does, but as a team we can achieve so much more. We found a way to help each other reach goals. We found it in teamwork.

My personal assistant, Michelle, doesn't care about her title in the company; she has many of them. She might be my assistant, but what most people don't know when they call Sam Glenn Presentations (my speaking company), is that she runs the entire company. She is the head Cheeto! When she started working for our organization years ago, it was part-time at first, and she did the small things, mostly the things nobody else wanted to do. However, she didn't complain and she did them well. She didn't sit around and wait for someone to tell her what to do next; she took initiative, got busy, and took our organization to a whole new level.

No one who works with our organization cares about his or her title in the company. Nobody cares who gets credit. The most important thing for us is that we are a team working toward a common vision. In order for us to achieve our goals and dreams, both personal and professional, it's up to us to work as a team. If someone is working only for himself or herself, then teamwork doesn't work.

Attitude in Action

Think about your relationships. Are they building you up, or down? If not up, then what can you do to network with more positive people?

Are there any relationships you need to distance from, or cut out? How do you think changing your relationships might change what you get from life?

15

A Kick in the Attitude Principle #13

Positive Leadership Inspires and Motivates Teamwork

None of us is as smart as all of us.

> —Ken Blanchard,
> author of *High Five: The Magic
> of Working Together*

You might agree that there are many, many definitions of leadership and an abundance of information about how to develop your leadership abilities. From what I know, however, all the resources in the world pale next to attitude. Great leadership starts with attitude. Leadership requires leading yourself first, and others will copy the way you lead yourself.

Become a leader who can inspire the best from others, moving them toward a common vision and doing it as a team. Otherwise, it's an "every man and woman for themselves" situation, and that's when things come undone.

Simple Tips for Inspiring and Motivating Teamwork

These are simple to do, so don't try and complicate them. The reason so many leaders end up wannabe leaders is that they complicate everything to the point that nothing makes sense. As a result, the team is no longer a team, and everyone is frustrated and seeking a direction in their own best interest.

Keep your leadership system simple, persistent, consistent, and always growing.

What I mean by this is you have to put new leadership concepts to the test. Not everything is going to work. You have to adapt and change your strategy and implement new ideas. What worked yesterday may not work today. This is how you build growth into your leadership arena.

"You don't need a TITLE to be a Leader."
—Mark Sanborn, author of *You Don't Need a Title to Be a Leader: How Anyone, Anywhere Can Make a Positive Difference*

Most people assume that when you get the title CEO, CFO, COO, or Boss, that you are a leader. The news is filled with people who had titles and handled them wrong—by choice. They used their teams not to benefit others, but rather themselves. I like what one guy said at a conference I attended: "Some of you work for a BOSS, which is Double S O B backwards." (Don't worry; you may get that later.)

The boss is not always the best leader within an organization. A longtime friend of mine works in recruiting. I admire her talent, "wow" attitude, and work ethic, which show. She gets the results she wants even in a tough economy. She works her leadership system. She inspires and connects with coworkers and clients. She doesn't own the company, but she works like she does. However, the owner of the company has a complicated definition of leadership, one that is driven by the news of the economy. My friend was asked to visit with the owner one day, as it was time for company reviews. She was expecting praise and a positive challenge to achieve more, but the owner of the company did not praise her or anyone in the company. Everyone who walked out of his office was either in tears or distressed. The owner criticized and informed everyone he was disappointed in their results and efforts.

Yeah, everyone is in tough times with the economy and stuff, but let me pose a question to you: Do you think this strategy was good leadership and moved people to unleash their best?

Instead of opening the door where people could thrive, feel good about their work, grow, feel secure, and work as a team, he blew up all that potential in a few short hours. The owner later found out that people were looking for other jobs. One employee was so distraught over how he was treated in the meeting that he called a lawyer to find out what his rights were.

The owner later had new meetings with everyone and apologized, but not sincerely—only to avoid trouble. His "non-leadership" system defeated him. He let his attitude get in the way, instead of creating a way for his team to work in a motivated environment. He then wasted company time and resources to try and repair what his poor leadership efforts created.

My friend, on the other hand, could have jumped ship or become negative, but instead she took it on herself to reassure people of their greatness and get the focus shifted away from what the owner had said, and back onto what was important.

Who is the real leader in the company I just described? Clearly, it is my friend. Leadership doesn't require a title. It requires positive effort put into action that brings out the best in others and moves them toward a common vision, working as a team. A leader helps others to do something they would not normally do on their own.

The Right Kind of Leadership Keeps the Lights On

A proactive attitude is the best antidote to competition in the marketplace. These times are competitive. It seems in these challenging times, a lot of people are setting off panic bombs that turn off the lights to forward progress. The panic bomb is when you respond to negative information in a negative way, making sure everyone knows about it and feels it just like you have. If you have to walk down a bumpy road, do complaints serve to smooth out the road? How about retaliation, or temper tantrums? Think on that for a moment.

If you interpret everything in a negative way, you set off panic bombs throughout an organization. Eventually a wave of doubt, uncertainty, and anxiety invades the workforce and productivity declines. If you want to keep the lights on, literally, it has to start with your attitude. Either you have a stable attitude, which this book is about achieving, or you have a sand castle attitude, which means when the tide comes in, you're all washed up and you take everyone with you.

One of my favorite stories is about a woman who runs a small salon. She would charge $30 for haircuts and they were good. One day someone informed her that a big chain haircut place was moving in across the street. Everyone got negative about the situation, except for her. She kept the lights on mentally. Everyone tried to justify why she should get negative: "They have commercials on TV, uniforms, marketing budget, name tags, etc."

She still, however, kept the lights on mentally. When you keep the lights on mentally, it keeps stress down, opens your mind to creative solutions, and best of all, provides an example for others to follow—how to respond in the face of adversity.

When the big chain store finally moved in across the street, they had a sign in the window that said, "Five Dollar Haircuts." Everyone on the other side of the street turned negative, except the woman who owned the salon. Someone informed her of the obvious, "They are charging $5 for haircuts and you charge $30. They are going to put you out of business!"

Now, you might agree, she did have a reason to panic and get negative. Right? Nope, she kept the lights on mentally and as a result, she got creative and put a big sign in her store window that read, "WE FIX FIVE DOLLAR HAIRCUTS!"

How is that for attitude in action?! In the words of retailing magnate J.C. Penney, "I would never have amounted to anything were it not for adversity." A true leader sees through adversity to find the next great opportunity.

Praise the Good Others Do

If you want to bring out the best in others, praise the good they do. Don't wait for a review, year-end banquet or the next e-newsletter to the company. Do it now and personalize it.

It's easy to call people out when they mess up, but if you do that all the time, people will be afraid to be innovative, think for themselves, and make something happen. If you see employees doing something good, write notes and put them on their chairs. Pull them aside for two minutes and praise them. Get personal and reinforce how valuable they are to the team. If you want to bring out the best in your team, do this leadership action—fast and a lot! This reinforces employees' motivation to keep up the work, making them feel valued and important and breeding loyalty and commitment.

Don't Listen Too Long to Your Critics

Not everyone is going to agree with you or your choices. If you try to please everyone, you will fail big-time. Are you going to make mistakes time and again? Sure you are. That's being human, and inevitably someone will always be there to let you know about your errors. You can dwell on them and personalize them to the point it affects your leadership efforts in a negative way, or you can learn from your mistakes, fix them, and move on.

Don't waste valuable time addressing your critics. I have been a professional speaker for 14 years now. I had no formal training and didn't set out to be a speaker. It just happened. I am going to toot my own horn; my presentation is TOPS! How do I know? Because I have been working on mastering it for 14 years, and just the other day Michigan Meeting Planners International named me Speaker of the Year, and I don't even live in Michigan. Not bad for a nighttime cleanup guy! I put a lot into my talks. I handwrite every single speech, and have written more than 2,000 talks. It's nice when an audience loves you, but to me it's about more than that. I want them to gain some valuable insights that will have a positive effect on their work and lives.

However, even though my team and I put a lot of effort into each presentation, with research and preparation, I know realistically that not everyone is going to connect with me or like my presentation. When I first started, a woman sent me a letter saying she didn't like my clothes or voice, and that my talk on attitude had no value in the real world. I sat down to write her a letter back, and when I looked at the clock, three hours had gone by and I still didn't have the perfect letter. I had spent three hours trying to write a letter to convince a negative person that I am good. Come on, what a waste of time. I can't get those three hours back. The issue wasn't with me; it was with her. I can't change her; only she can. I sent her a thank-you card with the words, "Thank you for your insights. Enjoy the sun today."

I am sure she was expecting a long letter back, and I am sure this little note jolted her system. There is a saying and I will say it again, "If you wrestle with a pig, you both get muddy and the pig likes it."

Don't waste your time on critics who are out to tear you down. Do what business philosopher Jim Rohn says: "Get ahead and not even."

Do Not Doubt Yourself, Doubt Your Limitations

We all have weaknesses and setbacks, but don't use them as an excuse to justify why something isn't working out. Have you ever met someone who has failed, and when asked about it, he or she blames it on something or someone else? The key to success and overcoming failures and adversity is in taking ownership of the picture. It's called responsibility.

Create a list of those you admire who challenged the limits. If you drive down any busy street in almost any town, chances are you will see a Wendy's restaurant. A guy by the name of Dave Thomas, who dropped out of the tenth grade, started from scratch and made his dream a reality. Did he encounter adversity and failure or have weaknesses? You betcha! But it did not determine his outcome.

What about Wal-Mart? If you read Sam Walton's book, *Made In America*, you will learn about all the challenges he faced getting Wal-Mart off the ground. It wasn't easy, but the setbacks and obstacles did not keep him from giving up.

I personally love to read about "Great Failures" who challenged the limits. They had every right to give up and offer up an excuse, but they doubted that limitation. Go to your local bookstore, and you can read about lots of great failures. Their stories let us know we are not alone and that if they can come back, get up, try again, and succeed, than we can, too. These sincere testimonies are not overnight success stories. These people likely encountered every emotion that comes with facing adversity, failure, and a personal encounter with some weakness. Take the time to appreciate and learn from those who have gone before us to encounter and overcome failure, achieving their desired successes. Ray Kroc, Abraham Lincoln, Thomas Edison, Colonel Sanders, Nelson Mandela—there are so many. Who do you admire? Can you follow their example and implement it into your leadership arena? Some may be well-known and yet some might just be local business people in your town. Value the wisdom that setbacks have taught them. Their gems may help you avoid pitfalls and possible failures in your life. Success leaves clues. Decipher and use them to challenge the limits.

Attitude in Action

Are your leadership actions bringing out the best in others? Is teamwork getting better, average, or worse?

Do something positive this week that lets your team know you are passionate about teamwork. Even if things seem grim throughout the organization, be an example that others can emulate and find strength in.

16

A Kick In the Attitude Principle #14

Always Take the High Road

The final forming of a person's character lies in their own hands.

—Anne Frank

A minister got on the public train system to go to his office downtown. He noticed that after he bought his ticket, the cashier attendant gave him back way too much change. As the minister rode to his office, thoughts danced in his mind about all the things he could do with the extra money. Because times were tough, he thought: *This is a good thing.* He even justified it as a gift from God: *Nobody will miss it, and plus, I am a good person. I can do something worthwhile with it.*

But it continued to drive him nuts all day, to the point where he had to leave the office to return the money. When he showed up to give the money back, he said to the cashier, "Young man, I am sorry, but you gave me too much change this morning."

The young man smiled and said, "No, I didn't. Yesterday I came to visit your church, and you preached on character and integrity. I just wanted to see if you were for real!"

Character is doing what is right; integrity is good character in action. We develop a solid sense of character from our repeated actions. To create a healthy character, we need to develop honest habits by repetitively practicing what is right.

The temptation to do the wrong thing will almost always present itself to you. So how do you react?

I remember walking through a hallway at a university which for some reason was full of pianos—around 20 of them, total. In front of the pianos was a sign, "Do not touch or play the pianos, or there will be consequences to pay." I knew right away that this sign meant business, and that whoever owned these very expensive instruments did *not* want you touching them. As I walked past each one, it took every ounce of my control not to reach down and hit a few bars. I wanted to; but I managed to avoid it. There was a girl in front of me, however, who gave in to temptation. She reached down and played a few notes; and as a result, a crazy piano guy screamed at her and chased her down the hallway.

Whether someone is watching or not, it's ultimately up to you to choose what you will do. Having a solid character is about being responsible. It's not about being popular; it involves doing what is right. Character is not defined by your looks or anything outside yourself. It is the core of what you stand for, what you do in tough situations, and how you respond to life. It is essentially who you are.

You can fool others some of the time, but you can never fool yourself. You have to live with your character; and you are the one who will reap its rewards. If you are doing what you say you will do and putting integrity into action, you don't have to look over your shoulder, cover your tracks, or worry about anything you do coming back to bite you.

Ask yourself: Can people trust me at my word? Will I really do what I say I will? If a camera was on me all the time for the world to watch, how would my life look? The key to having a solid character lies in knowing when it needs work; even if it's just fine-tuning. Take a moment and define the values and morals on which you promise yourself you'll stand—no matter what. The best way to think about this is to ask yourself: *What five traits would everyone who knows me use to define my character?* Or what five traits would you *like* them to use? Honesty? Loyalty? Kindness? Sincerity? Responsibility? Humility?

Once you define your character—or the character you strive to have—then begin living life in it. Practice it every day . . . in both the little and big things.

Attitude Kicker:

What to do if you have been bitten by someone's lack of integrity:

- Be a person of integrity at all times, even when you are tempted to seek revenge.
- Be ethical—do what is right.
- Respond with good wisdom—seek counsel and find options about how to respond. You don't want to stir a fire.

- Let go, get over it, and move on.
- Don't react with feelings (we tend to want to explode first), but rather act with principle.

Here are six character-building points:

1. **Practice integrity.** A short time ago, as I was walking off the airplane, I passed a seat on which someone had left a Mont Blanc pen. I am aware that these pens are extremely expensive; and as the last passenger off the plane, nobody would have known if I had taken it. I could have justified that I really needed a nice pen. Maybe it was meant to be. The universe was giving back to me in the form of a luxurious pen. But, nothing could be further from the truth. Because I make an effort to practice what I preach and live what I have defined, I opted instead to turn it in so that the owner could retrieve it (which I'll readily admit was a *little* bit hard!).

   Life will always present you with the opportunity to practice integrity. You likely really appreciate the value of integrity when it's given to you from someone else; so why not give it in return?

   A few months back, I left my wallet in the grocery cart at Costco. I had close to $300 cash in there along with all my credit cards; and I didn't realize it was missing until five hours after I left the store. I was fairly positive that someone had taken it; but I decided to check anyway. I called Costco, and an employee informed me that a woman and her daughter had returned it to the store. Aaah—such relief.

You truly experience the value of good character when something like this happens to you. Good character means knowing and abiding by the golden rule: *do unto others as you would have done to you.* A solid character counts for everything.

2. **Do what you say you will do.** If you make a promise, fulfill it; and if you break it, don't make an excuse. Let your yes be yes, and your no be no. Let your word be your bond.

3. **Respect others.** Respecting others means that you don't talk about them behind their backs; that you don't take advantage of others; and that you respect their background, race, and religion, realizing that we are all unique.

4. **Own your mistakes.** One of my biggest pet peeves is when someone makes a mistake but doesn't have the fortitude to own it. It takes more energy and time to find someone or something to blame than would likely be spent making the situation right. I believe that if you make a mistake, you own it, admit it, fix it if you can, and move on.

5. **Deal with letdowns.** Nothing breaks the heart faster than being let down by someone you trust. Words mean very little; but actions mean everything. When I'm tempted to dwell on the people and companies who have let me down, I stop and remind myself of business philosopher Jim Rohn's wise words: "Successful people don't spend time getting even; they focus on getting ahead."

6. **Practice forgiveness.** This may be the hardest one of all; but believe it or not, the value of forgiveness lies primarily

in how it makes you—not the person you are forgiving—feel. You need to find and make peace, so that whatever happened doesn't gnaw at you for years to come.

Sometimes people close to us will make mistakes that let us down. We need to find the courage to forgive, and not carry the weight of what happened. If there is a way to resolve the situation in a healthy way, then we must do that whenever possible. In fact, many current studies on forgiveness point to the fact that those who forgive are usually healthier. What better reason do you need?

Attitude in Action

Are you a person of your word 10 percent of the time? 50 percent? 99 percent?

Is there someone who wronged you? Does it still eat at you? What do you need to do to forgive and free yourself from it?

What does having a positive character mean to you? What does that look like?

17

A Kick In the Attitude Principle #15

Emotional Management—Tame Your Tiger or It Will Eat You

The attitude of self-control involves committing to thinking before you respond. It means responding in a healthy way, instead of reacting and creating regret.

Now more than ever, we live in reactive times. Spontaneous retaliation is easy. But it is infinitely more beneficial to your success and health to step back, think about your responses, and react to the situation or person in a constructive way.

People who exhibit self-control respond in a way that benefits them and the situation. They use wisdom power instead reactive power.

Coach Tony Dungy, who wrote the renowned book *Uncommon*, recognizes the need for patience and self-control in the way he approaches football, and it has led him to win Super Bowls as both a player and a coach, while also being highly respected as an inspirational icon. He values each man on the team, and treats each player with patience in order to nurture his best.

I remember a time when I was sitting at Chicago O'Hare airport waiting for my plane to board. The gate agent came over the intercom and said, "Ladies and gentleman, I am very sorry, but there is a mechanical problem that will cause a three-hour delay."

Even though I could hear the exasperated sighs of passengers, the overall attitude was, I would rather wait for three hours for the plane to be fixed than be in the air and discover there is a problem. Isn't that how most people would feel, after all? Well, immediately after the agent made the announcement, this little bald-headed guy walked up to the counter and let loose! He screamed, "I WANT THIS PLANE TO FLY RIGHT NOW! BLAH, BLAH, BLAH!"

He was so angry that I honestly thought his head was going to pop off. Now—do you think he contributed positively to the situation? Or do you think that he let his negative emotions take control? The answer is fairly obvious. We were all faced with a situation in which the only thing that we could control was our responses. This guy completely lost it—which didn't benefit anyone.

And guess what? As you might have imagined, the plane did not take off any sooner due to his outbursts. It left three hours later, just as the agent had predicted. This guy had himself a temper tantrum for no good reason; he didn't help himself, or the situation.

Losing control doesn't have healthy or positive benefits, and it usually makes people look pretty ridiculous. Have you ever seen a man have a temper tantrum and thought about how much you admire him? Hardly. Demonstrating self-control requires better emotional management. Let's say you have been stressed in some way and are fired up. Define some things that might calm you down. Use these soothing tools next time you get fired up. Listen to music, go for a walk, drink water, call someone, do anything to relieve the built-up negative emotions.

I am not telling you to suppress your negative emotions. You would turn into a volcano and eventually explode. I am only suggesting that you relieve the negative emotions in a more constructive way. I know that when I am stressed or on the brink of feeling negative, I hit the gym and walk on the treadmill for 30 minutes. I also have a few friends I can call, and when I do, they are ready to listen; but they also have a way of changing my attitude by interjecting some humor and encouragement. These actions defuse the negative bomb that might be ticking inside me. I become balanced, healthy, and in a better place to demonstrate self-control.

Attitude Kicker

We may not have a choice about what situations we find ourselves in, but we do have a choice about the attitude we bring to the situation.

Here are six quick actions you can take to help you tame your tiger.

1. Think before you respond.
2. Practice self-control or patience.
3. Do not take everything personally.
4. Never assume anything. Know the facts to determine the truth.
5. Seek to understand.
6. Do something else to take the focus off the situation for a bit.

Keith Harrell, author of *Attitude is Everything*, says we need to be pre-active. Preplan and practice your responses. For example, if you know certain people are going to push your buttons a certain way, preplan some responses that keep you from getting stressed out and limit your time with them. One woman, we'll call her Betty, wrote me about her clever pre-active story. Betty said every time she was in a meeting with a particular person who would always find a way to create chaos, she would ask for a break when things got heated, and be met with a "no." It was the woman's means of getting Betty under her control, and caused a waste of time, energy, money, and resources. So Betty got pre-active and planned a few responses so, if the meeting got out of control, they could take a break. The next time they were in a meeting and she started creating crazy chaos causing Betty to feel they needed a break, the woman again said, "No." Betty's pre-active response to add to that was, "We *really* need a break," while gently slipping some breath mints across the table. The look on the woman's face was priceless, and Betty got the break. In fact, Betty reported, "From that point on, anytime I asked for a break, I got it, because the woman thought it was her breath." Truthfully, it kind of was a case of "bad breath," because sometimes we need to come up for fresh perspective breath. You can't solve problems or be creative if you have a hot head. Your pre-active efforts don't need to involve Tic Tacs, but you can play out scenarios in your mind and think of some good responses.

To Be Good at Patience, Practice It by Starting Small

What you practice in your life will eventually return to you. Life requires us to respond to countless people and situations, and there are undoubtedly moments when we feel less than patient. Our patience is eroded every time we get worked up. In fact, people have been known to suffer heart attacks when getting intensely upset over given situations.

I remember a time when I was pulling out of a gas station behind a big rig. I was in front of a very impatient driver who wasn't able to see what was going on in front of me. I could see the truck's driver let someone pull out in front of him; I realized that if I pulled out, I would hit that person. It looked, however, like I was just sitting there not moving for no good reason. The driver behind me got impatient, and tried to make a statement by pulling around me. As a result, he got into an accident with another car.

If you do not practice patience, you practice regret. You may say or do something you wish you could take back.

I love the story of the father who practiced patience with his daughter. He walked out to see her brushing the dog's teeth with his toothbrush. Instead of yelling or reacting harshly, he calmly informed her: "Honey, if you are going to use Daddy's toothbrush to brush the dog's teeth, you need to tell Daddy."

The little girl responded, "Okay, Daddy. But, what about all those other times?" We always have a choice about how we are going to respond.

Four elements that can push our buttons and stir our tiger are:

1. Change
2. Challenges
3. The unexpected
4. Negative people

Attitude Kicker

Your attitude has the power to put out fires, and retune the orchestra. Play the tune right and you can create the right results.

When life throws you a challenging situation to which you have to respond, you need to ask yourself: "By the way I respond . . ."

Will I make this situation worse?
 or
Will I make this situation better?

Think of someone you admire who handles circumstances pretty well, and ask, "What would this person do?"

If you are reactive, the situation aggressively dominates you. If you are responsive (well thought out with a cool mindset), you control the situation.

Your choice of attitude is that one string you can and will play in every circumstance. A part of you may want to make it worse, because that's how you feel at the moment. We've all been there. I admit there are some situations in which I wish I was a bullfighter. But in the end, if you are reactive, you will hurt yourself and others.

Step away from the situation for a bit before you respond. Go slap some cold water on your face, take a walk, or eat some cheese (which actually does relax you). The reason we are told to count to 10 in tense situations is because it is a simple way to separate our minds from the situation, allowing ourselves to put out the mental fire.

If you are tired, stressed, or hungry and you encounter a change, challenge, something unexpected, or a negative person, you may not respond in the best of ways. You may just need to rest your mind and body for a bit. Take time to think it out.

It's unrealistic to expect that we will *never* get angry. Things are bound to happen in our lives that are going to upset us. It's okay to be angry about something, but it's important to keep your emotions from ruling your actions and producing regret.

Attitude in Action

What situations make you most angry?

How can you respond with more self-control?

Can you think of a situation, looking back, that you could have handled better?

18

A Kick In the Attitude Principle #16

FUN—A Simple Cure for Office Indigestion

What we are looking for, first and foremost, is a sense of humor. We hire attitudes.

—Herb Kelleher, CEO,
Southwest Airlines, as quoted in a *Fortune* magazine
cover story, May 4, 1994

One manager told me, "If we had fun in the workplace, we would get nothing done."

Another manager told me, "If we don't have fun, nothing gets done."

Which philosophy do you buy?

Which manager would you rather work for or with?

Which job would be more exciting to go to on Monday morning?

Is it really possible to have fun at work and accomplish great results? Research it for yourself, but there have been numbers of studies done on fun in the workplace. And you might be surprised to learn that people who have fun work better, harder, and get more accomplished.

Answer these six questions:

1. Is it fun to make money?
2. Is it fun when things get done?
3. Is it fun when everyone is working together better?
4. Is it fun when you feel good about life?
5. Is it fun for your family when you come home in a good mood?
6. Would it be fun if you carried around less stress?

If you answered yes to any of the preceding, then it's a safe assumption that fun at work is a good thing, right?

Although I covered this a bit in the chapter on humor, I believe in it so strongly that this chapter is dedicated to how to make the workplace fun. Fun creates positive mental and physical energy that transforms our attitude and shows up in the form of teamwork, enthusiasm, excellence, extra effort, loyalty, creativity, and innovation. Would teamwork, enthusiasm, excellence, extra effort, loyalty, creativity, and innovation make a difference in your organization?

What Light Is to the Bulb, Fun Is to Us

There is a fun book by Mike Veeck titled *Fun Is Good: How to Create Joy and Passion in Your Workplace*. Mike is part owner of six minor league baseball teams and highlights the value of injecting fun into the workplace, describing how it ignites passion and creativity, and transforms an entire workplace. After reading Mike's book, you can tell he is serious about fun.

I agree 1,000 percent. Everything suffers when you are not having fun. Teamwork, customer service, sales, productivity, quality, and leadership all suffer when there is a lack of fun. Fun is life. It's enthusiasm in action. Almost every phone conversation I have with clients or staff is infused with a little fun. My choice of fun is positive humor. If I can get you to laugh, that's fun for both of us. If you're having fun, you're gonna feel good about doing business with me. If you work with our company and are having fun, then you are going to enjoy what you do more.

An attitude of fun has many advantages. It has a way of burning off stress and calories.

You might argue, "Well, Sam, fun is great and all, but there are certain people here who would not allow fun into the office." I disagree. It may merely be their fear of the word *fun* that is creating the limitation. They probably think everyone will run around the office like kids with water guns. That's not true. At least, not in all cases. If you instead mention that you want to improve employee morale, retention, and productivity, you will likely experience a more positive reception. Who could turn down those things?

Fun That Functions in the Workplace

Let me outline how to put your workplace on track toward a little more fun, so you can experience some of the same results that so many fun organizations are benefiting from! Follow these simple principles, and watch your fun factor soar.

Fun Is Simple, so Keep It Simple

Fun can be as simple as going with your team out of the office for lunch.

You can do what one team did. They went to the zoo for lunch, and when they were leaving, they all ran to the parking lot screaming, "It's loose! Run!" I bet that freaked a lot of people out, but I also bet it was fun!

Establish a Fun Committee.

Paul McGee, PhD, states in an article which appears on his site LaughterRemedy.com, adapted from his book, *Health, Healing and the Amuse System: Humor as Survival Training*, "Every company has its own unique culture, and fun activities that work in one setting might not work in another. Establishing a fun committee not only helps assure that fun activities and events will actually be created; it assures that they will be appropriate for your company. This committee should rotate to keep ideas fresh and sustain ongoing commitment to fun on the job."

Create a Humor Bulletin Board

Encourage employees to contribute something fun or funny for a bulletin board. You can use a positive quote or cartoon. Make sure someone monitors this board for appropriateness of content. Collect cartoons and jokes that poke fun at the circumstances that cause negativity or conflict in the office. Consider checking out *Dilbert* for ideas. We interviewed Scott Adams, the creator of *Dilbert,* for our magazine, *Attitude Digest*, and he has some hilarious cartoons. They are very office friendly, but poke fun at what can be deemed negative.

Be Smart about Cultural Differences

With increased cultural diversity in many offices, managers must be aware of how humor affects various people, based on their backgrounds. Use discretion when looking for material.

Kick Off Your Meetings with Attitude Starters

Open or close meetings by sharing an Attitude Starter. Go to AttitudeVideos.com, which offers awesome short videos that you can use to kick-start your meeting with something fun, funny, motivational, and insightful. This is how you turn boring meetings "upside right."

Hold Contests with Prizes

Thousands of employees of a well-known health insurance provider get our magazine, *Attitude Digest*. This is a company in a serious business—helping people with health care needs— but they are also serious about something else. They value attitude in the workplace, believing that it is essential. It seems that every contest we put in our magazine, like Most Embarrassing Incident or Best Attitude at Work, is entered by several from this company, and many win. We also get some amazing letters about how they enjoy the humor and cartoons we place in the magazine. Several post them by their desks to brighten their mood.

I love the story of one woman who works in customer care with this company. She e-mailed us that she had read one of the humor articles and started laughing very hard just as the phone rang. She didn't want to pick it up laughing, but she could not help it. The person on the other line asked what she was laughing at, so she shared. The customer said, "I have had such a rough day and hearing you laughing just made my day."

I am not advocating answering the phone while laughing all the time, but sometimes being in that mood can help. If you called customer service anywhere, what kind of mood would you want them to be in: a.) Work is so uptight, someone just brought in a plant and it died by noon; or b.) Attitude makes a difference and I am in a good mood because work is fun.

Who do you think you're going to get the best service from? Think it over.

Food Is Always Fun

Brain food, mind candy, conceptual chewies—these are some good snacks that bring fun to the office. You can have a food contest once per month. Bring, bake, or buy your favorite dish. Here are some other favorites:

> Pizza and Diet Coke always say fun!
>
> Chocolate miniatures say yummy (come on, it's chocolate).
>
> Salsa and chips are impossible not to enjoy.
>
> Tootsie Rolls are chewy fun.
>
> Healthy veggies and dip—people love to dip!

Play Doh

Play Doh is a great toy to have on hand at work. I recently was quoted on this subject by *The Toilet Paper Entrepreneur*, Mike Michalowicz, in his blog. You'd think I am nuts, but when you're ADD you can lose focus quickly. Having Play Doh on hand to squeeze or mold odd creatures with while on a long conference call keeps me engaged in what I am doing.

Bernie DeKoven, aka Dr. Fun, says, "Toys are the first and easiest to implement. A good meeting toy is like a rosary or a set of worry beads. It gives the individual a way to relieve tension, engage the senses, and play."

Take a Break

It can be a 15-minute break or a retreat break. Either one can restore balance, relieve stress, and be as fun as you want.

The importance of fun is that it contains energy and life. Have you ever tried making an important phone call on a cell phone with hardly any battery life or reception? The same is true of people. We can't do what's important and be receptive if we have no energy. Fun is an attitude that helps achieve that goal. You don't have to overhaul the entire office overnight, but take small steps. You want it to be effective, not a circus.

> **Ten Funny Hypothetical Things to Do in Office Meetings Which Have Been Circulated Online (Don't actually do them. It's just funny to think about the reactions of people in your office if you did do them.)**

1. Take notes in finger paint.

2. At sensitive moments say, "Amen!"

3. Laugh uproariously at a quip that was made two or three minutes ago. Say, "Oh, *now* I get it!"

4. Wear a disposable paper face mask. Tell the group, "Hey, you don't want to catch what I've got!"

5. Check your watch very regularly, every 30 seconds or so.

6. Make a face like somebody beside you stinks.

7. Spill coffee on the conference table. Produce a little paper boat and sail it down the table.

8. Bring a noisy electric pencil sharpener. Sharpen your pencil every few minutes.

9. Remove your shoes and socks. Lay your socks on the table, turn each one inside out, and inspect them carefully. If anyone says anything about it, tell him or her, "Doctor's orders."

10. Every so often, duck under the table. Stare in horror. Pop back up and look really scared.

    Warning: If you plan to do these things on a consistent basis, you might want to have your resume dusted off.

Attitude in Action

Are you having enough fun at work?
What can your team do to implement more fun in your workplace?

19

A Kick in the Attitude Principle #17

Attitude Is Like Chalk Dust—It Gets on Everything You Touch

Success is not the key to happiness. Happiness is the key to success. If you love what you are doing, you will be successful.

—**Albert Schweitzer**

I believe that we are rewarded and promoted in life, and often beyond measure, when we *serve and treat others* with excellence. Excellence is that extra special quality that says, "We care enough to do the best we can with what we have."

It shows we are committed to providing the best for ourselves, and our family, friends, and customers.

All of us are in the business of serving, whether we work behind a desk, answer phones, travel, sell, preach, clean floors, or educate.

Excellence is doing the best you can with where you are, what you have, and who you are, while always being willing to grow and improve.

If you hate what you do, who you are, or where you are, I've got news—it shows. If you lack excellence, you will always sell yourself and others short. When you instead provide great service to others without taking advantage of them for personal gain, your rewards will be the best that life has to offer.

The online retailer Zappos.com prides itself on its devotion to customer service, describing itself as a service company that happens to sell a huge variety of shoes and accessories. CEO Tony Hsieh started a customer service team at Zappos.com to ensure that a response was granted to every customer e-mail. The company functions through the belief that providing their customers with a great shopping experience will result in a growth in sales over time. The company's focus remains on maximizing the service they provide rather than solely on maximizing profits.

Customer service and loyalty are at the forefront of the company's decisions and such a part of the company culture that the call center and headquarters are located in the same Las Vegas location. A new hire spends four weeks as a customer service representative before starting work to ensure the whole team is service-based and customer attentive. Customer service employees do not use scripts and are never pressed to keep calls brief. In other efforts to keep customers happy the warehouse is open 24/7, customers receive free shipping and return shipping, and most repeat customers are upgraded to free overnight or second-day shipping

What Is the Benefit of Giving and Creating Excellence?

Years ago, right before I went to college, I got a job working at a gas station. My manager had just come from another store to turn ours around. You could tell by his attitude that he was a superstar. He made others feel important and valued, and communicated the value of treating each customer with excellence. I can honestly say that he made my experience an enjoyable one.

Our uniform was a red smock. I didn't like it all. It was stained, and seemed like it had never been washed. So one day, instead of putting on the red smock, I decided to act with excellence and wear a nice shirt and tie. How often do you see this at a gas station? My professional look impressed my manager. He loved it and encouraged it. The difference was, when I wore the red smock, I didn't feel good about myself. I felt grungy and unattractive to others. But, when I put on that shirt and tie, I felt important. I had a sense of pride in my job, and was therefore more motivated to be excellent.

Things were going great at this job. The district and regional managers even complimented me on my shirt and tie. One day, they asked me if I had any desire to be a manager eventually. If I did, they said that I would make a great one. I told them that I'd had a great role model. My manager had been amazing.

But one Tuesday morning, it all changed. My manager got promoted again, after only six weeks. He had turned things around quickly, making our store exemplary with its clean, fast, and friendly service. I was excited to see him get promoted. His excellence paid off, as excellence always promotes and prospers.

The next day, we met the new manager. He was a whole different story. I knew it was a bad situation the moment he showed up—45 minutes late. He wasn't very friendly and his shirt was wrinkled with odd stains on it. He was not an example of excellence. He was the poster child for what not to do to be successful.

The situation grew worse when he pulled me aside for a little chat. He told me that I had to wear the required uniform, which was the red smock, and that he had better not catch me without it on. I said to him, "But doesn't the nice ironed shirt with no stains and nice tie that I am wearing look better?"

His response was, "It's company policy. Do it."

To say the least, I was depressed to put on that red smock again, but I did it. And as I did, my smile went away, my desire to do a good job vanished, and my excellence went into hibernation. At that point, I was only working for the money. My attitude was, *just give me my check and I am outta here.*

What was the result of this situation? After two weeks, the new manager got fired. By that point, it was time for me to go to college. I took with me a valuable lesson, and apply what I learned to this day. Just as my first manager's excellence had created good stuff in everything around him, fostering excellence starts a domino effect. Excellence is the ultimate form of greatness, creating the ultimate experience for others. This experience is so contagious that it also prospers and promotes you. You will be rewarded for your excellence.

Let me broaden the perspective on this with a few examples and see if you get my drift on this point.

Attitude Kicker

It's very simple. Your attitude creates an experience that people will want more of or less of. You determine which. If dealing with customers, think of them as money for a moment. Do you want more money or less money?

Have you ever been out to dinner and had the worst service ever? The servers didn't smile, and gave no eye contact. They instead looked at you like you were interrupting their day. Did the experience make you want to go back again? I am guessing the answer is an easy, "NO."

Perhaps you had something go wrong with a product and you wanted to fix it, but the representative with the company kept telling you, "We can't help you and here is why. We have a company policy and this is what it says. . . . "

It makes you want to freak out, doesn't it? Let's face it, we all get frustrated when we are neglected, treated badly, or have to listen to a company's policies about why we are out of luck. Bottom line, when you create a poor experience for others, you lose business and relationships.

On the flip side, when you create excellent experiences, you enrich your relationships, make your company look good, and expand your efforts or your business. You are a superstar.

How One Airline Lost $1 Million over a $50 Seat

I was in a travel bind in which I had to fly an airline that I normally don't use. I usually book American Airlines, as they have increased legroom for every seat, which appeals to me since, remember, I am 6'7". With this other airline, whose name I won't mention, we had a little unsettling situation: They had me in what they call an economy seat, which is a category defined by the fact that I don't fit. In fact, my legs press about four inches into the seat in front me.

Here's a little background on this alternate airline. They started having money problems, so in an effort to make some extra revenue, they decided to break up economy and create economy plus, which has a few more inches of legroom. The price tag on an economy plus seat is $50 extra. So, we called, talked to several agents, and were told the same thing over and over: "You will have to talk to the gate agent. We cannot help you with that. We can't release those seats to you unless you have status with us."

Status only occurs when you fly the airline all the time and your miles accrue. You get better treatment. But I didn't fly with them all the time, and my treatment was very poor.

When I checked in, I again explained the situation to the check-in agent, and again he said, "Talk to the gate agent." I talked with the gate agent, who said there were no seats left to switch me to, that I should have called reservations or talked with the check-in agent.

I was like, "*Aaah.* You have got to be joking."

When I got on the airplane and the doors closed, there was one economy plus seat open. Oh! They misled me, or were at least very disorganized! Instead of just moving to that seat, I politely asked the flight attendant, "Ma'am, as you can see, I am 6'7" and don't fit in this seat that I have. It's a very long flight; may I move to that open seat?"

She answered, "I am sorry, that seat is for people who pay $50 more. You need to call our reservations line to do that."

I said, "I called them. I talked to the check-in agent and talked to the gate agent, who told me there were no economy plus seats left. Can I just give you $100 cash, and you can let me move? You can even keep the extra $50 yourself.

She said, "I am sorry, there is nothing I can do."

Let's wrap up this experience, to clarify what happened. What did X airlines really communicate to me? Translated: "Sir, we don't value your business or care enough to create a fantastic experience for you. As a result, we would love to lose your business and that of those you know who hear about this experience."

This experience was sad because I am a great customer to have; but I am drawn toward great experiences, which they failed to create. And it cost them. When I estimated all of the flying I do, and added up what I paid per year for flights, and multiplied it by the next 15 years, this airline lost $1 million of business. Will it cost them more than $1 million? Maybe or maybe not, but it certainly didn't help them profit.

I predict that small, medium, and large companies would double, or even triple, in business without putting another dime into marketing or advertising, if they just made it a priority to work on creating an excellent experience for their customers. It's just that easy. People will pay more for a better experience, and it's simple. There is usually another place they can do business, and often right next door.

I recently spoke at an event where a manager from a major electronics retailer was in my audience. He heard me speak on this point and later approached me to talk about it. He informed me that he had recently been placed in charge of customer experience, and asked if I had any ideas for him. I looked at him, smiled and said, "I have some great ideas. But, they are simple. You have to realize that creating great customer experience doesn't have to be complicated." What happens today, and you see it a lot, is that companies complicate simplicity, and as a result, they lose customers, relationships, and profits.

I also remarked with great honesty that I had not experienced the best service in his stores, and knew a lot of other people who felt similarly. He smiled and said, "I know. That's why they put me in charge of creating customer experience."

I said, "Your chain did a major overhaul and changed the look inside their stores, which is very nice, but only cosmetic. The store may appear more professional, but if you don't offer a great experience for the customers, they will shop somewhere that does, even paying more for their experience."

We desire to return to places that create good feelings, and we will bring others with us. Sounds crazy, but it's true. We all have a choice in where we spend our time and money, and a big part of that is determined by where we get feel-good feelings.

I continued to talk to this manager about how his chain has a lot of young people working, which is great. But the store is not creating a wonderful experience or helping customers with challenges. It's not the teenagers' fault. It's the people who trained them.

One of the primary mistakes many companies make in training is in equipping their people to be top-heavy, using company policies and procedures but not their own personal insight, problem-solving skills, or innovation. This method is backwards and creates mere robots who can do nothing to help an outside-of-the-box situation. As a result, the customers with outside-of-the-box needs feel trapped. This is why I have great compassion for managers, because people always ask to speak to the manager. If we learned to treat customers right at step one, there would be less, "Let me talk to my manager, let me get the manager," and so on.

The goal in training employees should instead be to bring out their best, so that they are the best version representing the organization.

You can offer the best rates and deals, and have the most knowledge in the business, but the factor that matters most in determining whether you will create a successful and long-term relationship with a customer or client, or a terminated one, is the experience you create. It's about being attentive and active—projecting the attitude that you are putting the customer's needs ahead of all else. As the saying goes, "People don't care how much you know, until they know how much you care."

Are you beginning to see the value of this principle? It's huge!

Get a Clue

I am always alert to how people are representing their companies by the experience they create for others. I once visited a particular hotel in Florida—for the last time. I had heard it was a great hotel, and I am sure it might be, but based on my first-time experience there, I didn't care to stick around and find out if life got better.

This hotel looked nice when I arrived, but the experience I was about to encounter would lead me to seek other accommodations. I stood in line to check in for a very long time, and as customers were leaving the front desk in front of me, I noticed that there was not a single smile among them. They looked discouraged, a bit upset, and perplexed. And when I stepped up, I discovered why. The receptionist had no smile. She was not the slightest bit friendly. She didn't look me in the eyes. Instead, she was rude, and gave the impression that people had died and that she had killed them.

Then it hit me; so many companies go flop and lose business because people in the company create a "who died?" experience. I have loads of stories like this and I bet you have a few as well. It's really sad, because the difference between making someone's day, and ruining their experience, is just simple common sense. Building lasting relationships with people starts with creating excellent experiences for them. It's not that complicated, and yet so many companies and workers fail to deliver.

You don't get a second chance to make a great impression. If you blow up the bridge on the front end of the experience, you can expect it to get lonely after a while when no one crosses over to your side. Let's be real, if a worker is creating a poor experience, someone in leadership is usually not doing his job. Either someone has been ill-trained, or a policy is out of whack. And believe me, the customer won't wait around for things to get better; he will move along faster than you can say, "I am sorry." He won't be back, and he will take his friends with him.

Again, it boils down to attitude. The wrong attitude is poison to a relationship. The wrong attitude in your company or on your team is the elixir that prevents progress, and it doesn't take much to do it. You don't have to drink a gallon of poison for it to have an effect; just a teaspoon will do.

It may seem like I am complaining, and maybe I am a little, but it's frustrating at times when you are treated badly. How would you feel knowing that your son, daughter, wife, mom, or grandmother was treated very poorly? It would turn you red with anger.

You and I are the customers, and we have a choice in where we are going to invest our time and hard-earned money. The experience is everything. We will always seek out the best experiences, and when we find them, we will return to do it all over again. If you are the one creating the experience, and you care about your company and its success, remember this!

If You Aren't Sure What Else to Do, Sing

I was in the Newark airport and was a bit stressed out looking for the rental car location. The airport was crowded and I got a tense feeling just being there. But off in the distance I heard one guy singing. He was in charge of giving people information—where to go and how to get there. It was quite humorous and extraordinary. I walked over and asked how to get to the rental car place and he sang the directions. What experience did he create for me? A positive one that I will never forget. I smiled and laughed and walked away feeling stress free. Not only did that guy make me feel good, he made the Newark airport look good to me, and to all those other travelers. Now, when I fly there, I actually look for that guy.

Some Just Need a Simple Nudge to Create Greatness

Sometimes, people in service just need a little insightful nudge to change a bad situation into a better one. I was checking into the Four Points Sheraton hotel and my room wasn't ready. I didn't have a car or anywhere to go and they said it would be about an hour's wait.

I noticed that other people were also just standing around and waiting. Some people were very upset. The atmosphere was tense and the manager was getting an earful from several patrons.

So, I jumped in to relieve the manager. I pulled him aside and explained that he could turn this around in less than two minutes. He could create a better experience for everyone standing around, and get back to preparing rooms instead of fielding complaints. I said, "You have people who are just waiting around by the front desk, frustrated. They are tired and ornery. They have nowhere to go, and the information you are giving them is not helping the situation. It's only making them more upset. I notice you have a restaurant connected. Why not take everyone's luggage, bring it to their rooms when they become ready, and treat everyone waiting to your best piece of pie and a cup of coffee? It will only cost you a few bucks, but instead of starting their experience on a sour note, you can turn this situation around. You will make yourself and Sheraton look good. These people will go from being frustrated to loving you. What do you think?"

The manager replied, "That's a really good idea! Let's do it." The response was amazing. The tension went away and smiles appeared like a rainbow after a stormy day. It worked.

Sometimes situations may not start off on the right foot, but you have the ability to turn them around if you so desire.

If you are going to create an experience for others, why not make it a great one that enriches your relationship with them? The difference is that poor experiences repel people, while excellent experiences attract people. If you want to be a superstar in any relationship, and be successful for your company, then you have to grasp the concept that your attitude creates the experience for others. Your attitude can take you up or down. If promotion and growth is your ambition, then you need to start by creating the right kind of experience for others.

Brand Yourself with Your Experience

It may seem like I hit the business aspect hard, and I did, but the same principle applies to our personal relationships. Your attitude creates an experience for your family and friends. Your attitude touches people every day. It colors your world. When you spend time with your kids, it creates a memorable experience. When you're married and you still go out on dates (with your spouse!), that creates an awesome experience. When you give a smile, make a friendly call, send flowers, write a thank-you card, clean the house, do the little things, big things, and extra things, it all creates excellent experiences.

　　Your attitude either brings people up or down. The question you have to ask yourself is, "How much do I value my relationships?" If you really care, then you will take the time to infuse your best attitude into them. People do not want to be around someone who is like a bucket of ice water all the time. Be consistent in the experiences you create for others. If you strive to be excellent in this area, you will reap many rewards.

You Are Either a Duck or an Eagle

I credit Dr. Wayne Dyer for opening my eyes to this insightful perspective. He talks about how in life, we will encounter one of two types of people—a duck or an eagle. An eagle is a solution finder. It understands the value of creating a great experience. It goes above and beyond. It doesn't talk down to you, or insult your intelligence. It has a desire to make your day. If something is wrong, it will own it and attempt to fix it. It has an extraordinary vision for success.

A duck, on the other hand, is a robot in action. It doesn't take initiative and is not terribly helpful. It sees a dead end before it sees a way up, over, and around. It will find someone to blame. After a while, all you hear from it is a cranky "quack, quack, quack." Ducks are who cause us have to ask for someone else to help us, because we know that they can't or don't really want to.

My question to you is, when it comes to your treatment of others, are you a duck or an eagle? How do you become an eagle?

You Can't Please Them All

The effort to create a great experience for someone might not always turn out the way you want. Things do go wrong. Something might happen that is out of your control or not your fault. Whatever it is, be authentic and sincere about the situation. Own it, apologize, and try to fix what you can. Then do what you can and move on.

I have had many situations with companies or people wherein the situation or experience was going badly, but they turned it around. They didn't play the blame game or treat me poorly; they did what they could to fix the experience and make it up to me. In exchange, I left the situation in most cases with even more respect for those companies or individuals.

But sometimes an apology won't seem to be enough to resolve a conflict. There are times when you simply need to move on. If you authentically care about building healthy relationships, expanding your business, and making your company look good, it's important to know that you won't be able to please everyone. Bill Cosby once said, "I don't know the key to success, but I do know the key to failure is trying to please everyone."

If, despite your most sincere efforts, you are unable to make someone happy, you may have a customer who is impossible to please or be in a dysfunctional relationship. You will know this is the case if no matter how hard you try to create a great experience for the person, he or she always finds something negative in your efforts. In these cases, it's important to know that the issue isn't with you; it's with them. They are acting as mere complainers focusing on the bad. One hundred things may go well, but if one thing goes wrong, they are on it like white on rice.

It's also important that you not beat yourself up emotionally when they try to. If you have done the best you can, then that's all you can do. It might mean that the relationship wasn't meant to be, and that in order to be healthy, you both have to go your own separate ways.

When I first started my speaking business, I trained my staff to treat our clients like superstars. My goal was to create a different experience than anything our clients had known. But, every now and then, we encountered some very rude people. My first thought was, *they must really need my program badly.* But in one situation, a client used such explicit language and was so rude to my assistant over something very small, that I had to step in and say, "This is not right. While I value your business and have a desire to create the best experience for you, you are not allowing that to happen. Speaking down to someone with disrespectful words is not okay. We will not be able to do business with you."

Was that hard to do? Very. But, allowing it to continue was unhealthy, and the emotional headache began to affect morale. Sometimes, you have to let go and press on.

Ten simple ways you can act as an eagle, creating great experiences for others:

1. **Do your best with what you have, what you know, and where you are.** Don't make excuses: "*Well if only I was this*" or "*If only I had that*" or "*If only they didn't do this.*" These kinds of excuses will keep you from your best. Play the cards you have been dealt, but play them with confidence. Play them with your best effort.

   Before I graduated from high school, my goal was to get a college scholarship. I went to a few basketball camps to see if I could get noticed, but what I discovered is that I didn't look different than any of the other athletes, and my level of talent wasn't better than anyone's around me. I could tell that some players were on their way to the pros. My first thought was that maybe I should go sit in a corner or pack up and go home.

   Then I remembered something my coach shared with me: "Just give the best of who you are, and that's all anyone can ask. If you don't, you will sell yourself short."

   I went out there and gave the best of who I was, what I had, and what I knew. Mind you, I did have some talent and ability, so I used every ounce I could. And I did something else: Instead of trying to compete eye for eye against those who were more talented, I strove to excel past them. Excelling in this way involves recognizing that you have weaknesses, but not allowing them to control you, instead capitalizing on your greatest strengths.

   And it worked in my favor. I couldn't rely on my talent alone. I had to hustle on the basketball court if I was going to get noticed. I cheered on my teammates. I brought a spirit to the game that made me stand out. While most players jogged from one training station to another, I flat out ran like I was being chased in the dark. I may have even looked a little crazy, but at the end of the day, I had coach after coach asking me to visit their school. They liked my hustle, my attitude, and my spirit.

2. **Care enough to give your best.** Mac Anderson, who I mentioned earlier, believes attitudes are truly contagious, and that from time to time we all need to ask ourselves if our attitude is worth catching. Imagine going to the dentist. You want her to care enough to be gentle. If you or a loved one has surgery, you want the surgeons to care enough to perform at their peak. When you hire people to build your home, you want them to care enough to create it to the best of their ability. When we don't care enough, we hurt others and ourselves. When we give a poor performance because we didn't care enough to give our best, the result is that people get ripped off, and we rip off ourselves. Could you imagine getting married to someone who only loved you about 67 percent, and not 100 percent? What if your favorite football team went out and just gave 50 percent of the effort they were capable of giving? If they were okay with being just average, wouldn't you feel ripped off as a fan?

   Years ago, a story was told about a builder who had been working more than 30 years and was about to retire. He was asked to build one more house before his retirement. He felt like his employer had not been very fair to him over the years, so on this particular house, he decided not to be as careful. He instead wanted to wrap it up quickly and cut corners.

The finished house was not a work of art; it was a less than average home. The builder didn't care. He was retiring and thought his employer could deal with the issue from here on out.

And then the builder got the surprise of his life. His employer informed him that because of all his hard work and effort over the years, to reward him, the house was a gift to him.

Do you get the idea why it's important to care? When we don't care, we don't progress.

3. **Like what you do.** When you like what you do, you will have more passion for giving your best to others. This point ties the other two together. When you enjoy what you do, everybody wins.

4. **Smile and be friendly, even when others may not.**

5. **Be attentive.** Don't try to do two things at once half-heartedly. Do one thing at a time, and do it awesomely.

6. **Do what you say you will do.** If you can't do something, find someone who can.

7. **Go above your customers' or loved ones' expectations.** Do something to wow them. We all have wow power. Define yours and use it often.

8. **If you make a mistake, own it, admit it, apologize for it, and do what you can to correct it.** When you blame others you demote yourself. You close the door to advancement—financial, new opportunities, new position, whatever you can think of that is forward for you.

9. **Give your best.** If you order a baked potato, you don't want it half-baked. So, give people your best, not a soggy, half-baked potato.

10. **If someone is upset or has a complaint, don't take it personally.** He or she is upset for a reason; your job is to help overcome that reason. Be understanding and sympathetic to the situation. Don't simply recite your policies, if dealing with a customer, or your judgment, if dealing with someone closer to you. Treat others how you want to be treated, or how you want your dearest loved ones to be treated. How you would want your mom, grandma, kids handled if they got a bad deal or something went wrong. If I ever saw my mom, grandma, or children mistreated or not helped, it would get me fired up. So remember this the next time you are helping someone.

The experience you create for others determines your successes or your failures in business or relationships. Over the years, I have seen people grasp this concept and, as a result, they flourish, prosper, and partake of the best results that life has to offer. On the other hand, those who create poor experiences dismiss themselves from life's abundant rewards.

Attitude in Action

On a scale of one to ten, where is your attitude of excellence in your personal relationships, health, and in your work?

What could you do to exhibit more excellence in what you do? Only you know what must be done to become excellent. *Remember, the experience you create for others will determine whether they run from you or run to you. This experience will also determine whether you rise up, or slip down.*

20

A Kick In the Attitude Principle #18

What Will Your Legacy Be?

If you want to touch the past . . . touch a rock.
If you want to touch the present . . . touch a rose.
If you want to touch the future . . . touch a life.

—**Unknown**

Attitude means *nothing*—until you put it into *action*!

What will people remember of you?

What will your legacy be?

If there is one action I know of that restores an eminent energy of hope and enthusiasm into our very existence, it is when we reach out to make a difference. That's the core of what creating a legacy is all about. It involves bringing the greatness of who you are to someone who needs it. Empowering ourselves starts by reaching out to empower others. What we send out really does return to us multiplied. Proverbs 11:25 says, "He who refreshes others, will himself be refreshed."

Sometimes it can be so easy to get discouraged in our efforts to make a difference. But the questions you have to ask yourself are: What will my legacy be? What do I want it to be?

What will others remember of me when I am gone? What actions did I take to make someone's day or life better, or bigger? We will all be remembered for something.

Years ago, I wrote a poem that circulated on the Internet, titled "Butt Prints in the Sand." It got such a good response that I followed it up with my first book, titled *Butt Prints in the Sand . . . No More.* I think when we look back on life, we are going to either see butt prints in the sand or footprints. Take that however you want, but the point is, what will you see? To see footprints means you got up, tried, gave your best, didn't settle for average, put the best of who you are into play, and that's what counts. To make butt prints means you accepted your circumstances as is, made excuses, were lazy, and didn't care enough about yourself and others to make a positive impression in time with the greatness that resides within us all.

Three Things You Need to Know about Making Footprints

1. *We all have something to give.*

We each showed up with a unique and special gift in life, which is our ability to make a difference in the lives of others. Making such a difference can happen with such simple acts as a smile, a kind word, listening, and so on.

Years ago, I pitched a mega-million dollar idea to McDonald's that got shot down faster than you can say Big Mac. You can tell me what you think. I told them they could create a movement with the Happy Meal. The Happy Meal is an attitude in a box. It's not so much about what's in the box as what the experience of the box represents. So many people are having tough times these days and could use something to make them happy. When I got the letter of rejection in the mail, it said, "Happy meals are for kids. Adults would not be interested in this."

Are you kidding me? Imagine a commercial. Someone is daydreaming about those special moments as a kid and a Happy Meal is in that memory. Then, to connect to the moment, you go get one.

I remember being in McDonald's when my two brothers and I were fighting over what we wanted, and Dad was shouting, "Shut up! You will have a Happy Meal and be happy about it!"

And he was right—we were. Dave and Busters is brilliant at this. Have you seen their commercials? It's about bringing your inner child out, which they call "Fun." You see adults being carefree and enjoying life. I think we all need an attitude in a box some days, would you agree?

But, in the business world, imagine this commercial: Someone is having a hard day at the office. You've tried everything to lift this person's spirits, but then you drive by and see those golden arches. Suddenly it hits you: "I would like to get him a Happy Meal."

Your coworker comes back to his or her desk and there sitting front and center is a Happy Meal. The colleague looks around confused and then reads the note: *"You seemed a little down, so I thought you needed a Happy Meal. If you eat it, it will make you Happy. P.S. If you still feel really negative after eating this, there are five more Happy Meals in the company refrigerator."*

Personally, I can connect to this image more than to one of people frolicking in the streets, dancing and spinning around with Big Macs in their hands. Have you seen these commercials? If I danced around with a smile and a hamburger in one hand in my town, people might call the police or who knows what.

Making a difference is about creating an impression that sticks in time. Even if people mock it (as I just did with the dancing commercial), it can be a real good thing because it sticks.

Years ago, and some of you might remember this, because I do, there was a commercial in which a little boy was at summer camp and he started crying, *"You know what I miss? I miss McDonald's French fries."* And everyone agreed and started crying. My family would say that line all the time. I would hear people in McDonald's waiting to order singing that, too. We mocked it, but it stuck. It was funny, yet it always put the impression of hot, golden, salty fries into your mind.

So, I shared my Happy Meal Concept with an audience I was speaking to and someone listening put it into practice. He and his wife were at the store and the cashier was very rude to them.

You always have a choice when you encounter a negative attitude. You can simply move on, or you can stop and use your difference-making abilities to draw out the best in others—even though it goes against your heated emotional feelings in the moment.

On the surface, you may encounter a negative and defeating attitude in someone else, but if you seek out the person's best, you can find it. You can take on the attitude of Luke Skywalker in *Return of the Jedi*, when he kept telling his father, Darth Vader, "I know there is good in you, Father."

Sometimes a person's goodness is submerged by hard times, frustrating coworkers, a situation at home—who knows. But, as a footprint maker, you have the ability to resurface someone's best.

So getting back to the story, this guy and his wife went to McDonald's to buy the rude cashier a Happy Meal. The wife wanted to rant about his rudeness to the manager, but the husband said, "Let's test this and see what happens." They got back in line, and when they stepped up, the cashier was still in a rude mood.

They placed the Happy Meal down, and the cashier looked at them, asking, "What's this?"

"It's a Happy Meal," they replied. "You looked like you could use one tonight. If you eat it, it will make you happy."

The cashier just about melted. His hard-looking face softened. His shoulders dropped and the tension dissolved. He smiled, and with tears in his eyes, said, "I am sorry if I treated you badly. It's been a hard day. Nobody has ever done anything like this for me before. Thank you."

This fellow told me that every time he goes to that store and checks out, that guy smiles and treats his wife and him with the best he has.

2. *Give the gift of you.*

We all have something to give that can make a difference. Each of us can lend a hand, give a hug, give of our time, make a phone call, get involved, clean toilets, sit with someone and listen. It all makes a difference!

Attitude Kicker

Some cause happiness wherever they go; others whenever they go.

—Oscar Wilde

Who you are makes a difference. Don't keep your music and gifts locked up; open up and let the colors of who you are and what you have to give touch the life of another. Take a moment to think about what you have to offer that will make a positive impression in time. If people have left you out in the dark or made you feel worthless and useless, I have some news for you—they are in the wrong! They are too busy and blind to see you for who you really are. You have a gift you can give the world. Maybe it's your smile, kind heart, generous ways, or thoughtfulness. Making a difference doesn't take much. It only requires an attitude of willingness to step out, step up, and step forth to make a difference. Think about something amazing someone did for you. Didn't it feel great and touch your heart? Why not do that for someone else?

The difference between making footprints or butt prints in the sand is that one has you looking back saying, "I am glad I did," while the other has you saying, "I wish I had." Nobody wants to look back and feast on thoughts of regret. We are all valuable, with incredible gifts ripe for making an impact. We simply must step out and use them, rather than sit down and ride this life out.

I have been on the receiving end of someone else's graciousness. The first Christmas after my parents divorced, it was just me, my two brothers, and Mom. We didn't have much money, yet someone got us a box of food for the holidays. And while it was humbling to accept, we did. I remember my mom's tears, and how thankful she was that someone had lent a helping hand during such a hard time.

What three things would best describe your gifts of making a difference?

1. _____

2. _____

3. _____

3. *Get involved.*

One of the best ways to start making a difference is to get involved in a worthy cause. What are you passionate about? What do you feel called to act upon? Whatever positive change you want to see in the world, get active in a cause that addresses that issue. Maybe it's the fight against breast cancer; if so, there are many groups waiting for your help and energy. If you want to help dreams come true for children with cancer, you may choose to work with the Make A Wish Foundation. There are many great organizations in need of your help or donations.

Years ago, I got involved by doing an internship at a summer camp in Marshall, Indiana. What I had in mind and what they had planned, however, were two different things. They wanted me to clean dishes and bathrooms in all the cabins. After one day of cleaning bathrooms, I reevaluated my passion to make a difference that summer. I didn't want to clean toilets. I wanted to be among the people to talk and engage in what I considered meaningful activities.

I was about ready to quit, when the camp director opened my eyes to what it really meant to make a difference. My attitude had been wrong. As a result, I was seeing the worst in the situation. He told me point blank, "If you don't clean those bathrooms, then who will? And if you only do an average, get-by job, then does that really make a difference?"

The lesson in this for me was that making a difference can start by something as seemingly small as picking up a piece of trash from the ground, or filling in where it's needed most. And no, these may not always be the most glamorous jobs, but if you have a real desire to make a difference, then you will adopt the right attitude that gets the task done well.

I did just that. I got passionate about cleaning the bathrooms. In fact, I started cleaning the bathrooms with the expectation that whoever used them would feel the difference. I put up positive quotes on the mirrors and did a job that had my supervisor wanting to hire me full-time. The experience changed my life, and altered my outlook on what it really meant to make a difference and create a legacy.

Attitude in Action

What unique qualities do you possess that you can expand upon in creating your legacy?

Is there a group that you want to get involved with?

And Now for a Wrap Up

If I can leave you with any one thought, it is to seize each day to the fullest. You're gonna make mistakes, life is gonna kick your butt, but don't give up.

When I was in the eighth grade, we had a school dance. I remember being so scared of what others would think if I danced. I had one friend who stood by me for an hour or so while others seemed to have the time of their lives. My friend could not contain himself and finally just ran out to the dance floor and moved like a monkey on way too much caffeine.

I remember everyone saying, "Sam, come on! Dance. It's fun. Who cares what anyone thinks? Just move."

And then I remember hearing the DJ announce, "Okay, this is the last dance. Make it count."

I didn't dance because I was too afraid. I think about that moment and what I missed.

I don't want you to miss out, too. Life is not a dress rehearsal—this is the show. This is *your* show. Make each day count. Don't let laziness, fear, or adversity seize your daily gift—life. Helen Keller was right: "Life is a great adventure."

I can't make you have a good attitude or build your success; only you can. I have given you some useful tools to keep you on the positive track and to keep that *kick* strong within you. When you feel yourself getting drained, take time to recharge. When people you care about hit a wall, offer them a

"Kick in the Attitude." They will love you for it—maybe not at the moment, but when it sinks in, it works.

Attitude Works! If you believe that, be a living example that Attitude Works! Give your attitude life and put it into action.

I believe we need to affirm simple truths every day, so I have shared this affirmation with several of my family and friends who now read it every day. I hope you get from it what I have.

And if we happen to meet one day, let's grab some coffee.

The Attitude Guy™'s Affirmation

Read this to yourself quietly or loudly every day:

Attitude is a choice.

It is my daily choice!

The attitude I choose to use when engaging with life will determine my experiences.

It will determine . . .

Where I go,

What I achieve,

and

What I attract.

Without thinking too long about this, what three choices could I make right now to make my life worse?

Okay . . .

What single choice could I make right now to make my life better?

Which type of life do I prefer—one that is better, or worse?

For most, the answer is a no-brainer. Let's assume you are one of 99.9 percent of people, and you prefer a better life. How do you start?

Life gets better when I get better.

If I desire better experiences for my life, I must choose a better me, which begins by choosing a better attitude—it's that simple!

My attitude is the starting point to

Better relationships,

Overcoming challenges,

Achieving dreams,

And getting the best out of life and myself.

—— Attitude in Action Plan ——

Use this area to take notes on the Attitude in Action questions at the end of each chapter. Expand at will to make this your own "kick in the attitude" journey! Here are a few questions to get you started, in case you are antsy.

What five things am I most grateful for?

_____

_____

What are my unique qualities?

_____

_____

What is my greatest strength in life?

_____

_____

What is my plan for my goals and dreams?

_____

_____

What five things do I want to achieve in the next year?

_____

_____

Who is someone I admire?

_____

What helps me deal with stress?

_____

_____

NOTES

Index